Wasatch Eleveners

WASATCH ELEVENERS

A Hiking and Climbing Guide to the 11,000-foot
Mountains of Utah's Wasatch Range

RANDY WINTERS

THE UNIVERSITY OF UTAH PRESS
Salt Lake City

The Defiance House Man colophon is a registered trademark of the
University of Utah Press. It is based upon a four-foot-tall, Ancient
Puebloan pictograph (late PIII) near Glen Canyon, Utah.

19   18   17   16   15   14   2   3   4   5   6

LIBRARY OF CONGRESS CATALOGING-IN-PUBLICATION DATA
Winters, Randy, 1964-
  Wasatch eleveners : a hiking and climbing guide to the 11,000-foot mountains
of Utah's Wasatch Range / Randy Winters.
        p. cm.
  Includes bibliographical references.
  ISBN-13: 978-0-87480-864-3 (pbk. : alk. paper)
  ISBN-10: 0-87480-864-2 (pbk. : alk. paper)
  1. Hiking—Wasatch Range (Utah and Idaho)—Guidebooks. 2. Wasatch Range
(Utah and Idaho)—Guidebooks. I. Title.
  GV199.42.U82W378 2006
  917.92'2—dc22   2006000182

www.UofUpress.com

Interior printed on recycled paper with 30% post-consumer content.

Contents

Tables

Maps

Acknowledgments

I would like to thank my wife, Melissa, for her love and support during this endeavor. Without her this book would not have been possible. Kids have a unique perspective on life, and my son Jeremiah is no exception. Special thanks to him for being the other key member of my support team. Finally, thanks to my dad. Life cheated him by taking it from him prematurely. I have yet to meet or know a better man. He will forever be my hero.

Preface

Several books have been written about hiking in Utah, and some of those books include hikes and peaks in the Wasatch Mountains. Mount Timpanogos even commands its own book. While most of these books include generic descriptions for the 11,000-foot peaks of the Wasatch, not one of them includes all of them or provides detailed and comprehensive route descriptions. I have written this book specifically for climbers and peakbaggers—a peakbagger being defined as anyone who likes to climb every peak on a list of peaks. The author has climbed every peak, scrambled every ridge, and traveled every trail in this book. Every peak has been climbed multiple times and every route and peak was climbed within a year of this writing to ensure the most accurate information possible.

In addition to providing a comprehensive guide to the 11,000-foot peaks of the Wasatch, this book serves one more purpose. It has been written to educate and better prepare hikers and outdoor enthusiasts regarding the dangers and risks involved in hiking and climbing the Wasatch's highest peaks. Each year dozens of Search and Rescue missions are launched to rescue stranded or injured hikers and climbers. Some of these rescues are necessary, as was the case with my friend who suffered a life-threatening fall while attempting the Cottonwood Traverse. However, many rescues could be prevented if hikers were properly educated and prepared, and appropriately assessed risks. Risk can never be eliminated, but it can be mitigated. Many underestimate the effect of higher altitudes and the level of physical fitness required on some routes. Others underestimate the duration of their hike, the amount of water required, and the potential impact of bad weather, while grossly overestimating their ability to make sound judgments. Proper preparation and a sound understanding of the Wasatch Mountains will help you respect and enjoy them more safely.

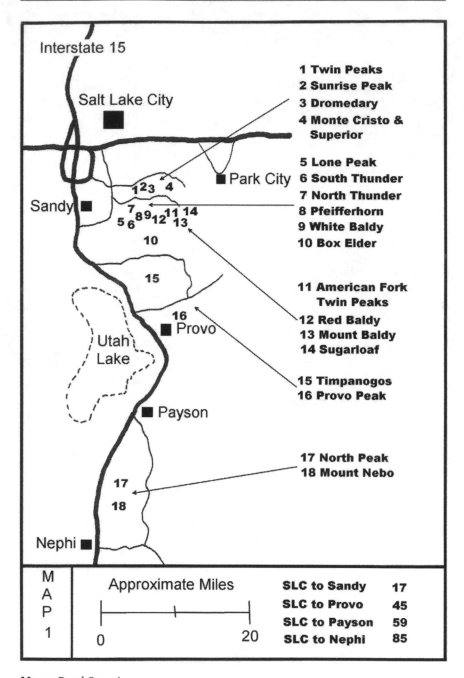

Interstate 15

Salt Lake City

Park City

Sandy
1 2 3 4
7
5 6 8 9 12 11 14
13
10

15

16
Utah
Lake
Provo

Payson

17

18

Nephi

1 Twin Peaks
2 Sunrise Peak
3 Dromedary
4 Monte Cristo &
   Superior

5 Lone Peak
6 South Thunder
7 North Thunder
8 Pfeifferhorn
9 White Baldy
10 Box Elder

11 American Fork
   Twin Peaks
12 Red Baldy
13 Mount Baldy
14 Sugarloaf

15 Timpanogos
16 Provo Peak

17 North Peak
18 Mount Nebo

M
A
P
1

Approximate Miles

0   20

SLC to Sandy   17
SLC to Provo   45
SLC to Payson   59
SLC to Nephi   85

MAP 1. *Road Overview*

TABLE 1. *Wasatch Eleveners Checklist*

✔	GROUP	CHAPTER	SECTION	PEAK	ELEVATION
	Nebo	5	18	North Mount Nebo	11,928
	Nebo	5	18	South Mount Nebo	11,877
	Nebo	5	18	Middle Mount Nebo	11,824
	Timp	4	15	Mount Timpanogos	11,749
	Timp	4	15	"South" Timpanogos	11,722
	Resort	3	11	West American Fork Twin Peak	11,489
	Resort	3	11	East American Fork Twin Peak	11,483
	Timp	4	15	"North" Timpanogos	11,441
	Resort	3	11	"South" American Fork Twin Peak	11,391
	Timp	4	15	Unnamed 11,383	11,383
	Timp	4	15	Unnamed 11,347	11,347
	Twin	1	1	East Broads Fork Twin Peak	11,330
	Twin	1	1	West Broads Fork Twin Peak	11,328
	Lone	2	8	Pfeifferhorn	11,326
	Lone	2	9	White Baldy	11,321
	Twin	1	2	Sunrise Peak	11,275
	Timp	4	15	Unnamed 11,288	11,288
	Lone	2	5	Lone Peak	11,253
	Nebo	5	17	North Peak	11,174
	Resort	3	12	Red Baldy	11,171
	Resort	3	14	Red Top Mountain	11,171
	Lone	2	6	South Thunder	11,154
	Lone	2	7	North Thunder	11,150
	Lone	2	8	Unnamed 11,137	11,137
	Twin	1	4	Monte Cristo Peak	11,132
	Twin	1	3	Dromedary Peak	11,107
	Lone	2	10	Box Elder Peak	11,101
	Resort	3	13	Mount Baldy	11,068
	Timp	4	16	Provo Peak	11,068
	Resort	3	14	Sugarloaf Mountain	11,051
	Timp	4	16	"East" Provo Peak	11,044
	Twin	1	4	Mount Superior	11,040
	Resort	3	11	"East" American Fork Twin Peak	11,007

Introduction

Wasatch Mountains Overview

The Wasatch Mountains are located in the western range of the Rocky Mountains. They are a product of twenty million years of geologic faulting, volcanic activity, and glaciation. Stretching across Utah from Bear River in the north to Mount Nebo near Nephi in the central part of the state, their peaks dominate the skyline in the most populous portion of the state. Most elevations along the Wasatch range between 9,000 and 11,928 feet, the highest being Mount Nebo. The majority of Utah's population has chosen to settle along the range's western front. The mountains were a vital source of water, timber, and granite for early settlers. Today they continue to serve as the primary source of water for the populous Wasatch Front and provide year-round recreational opportunities to residents and visitors alike.

White Pine Lake with Twin Peaks Wilderness as background

Climate

Because of Utah's mid-continent location, it experiences wide temperature variations between seasons. Climates in Utah also vary greatly with elevation. During winter and spring most precipitation comes in the form of snow, with a deep snowpack accumulating in many of the higher elevations. Some areas in the Wasatch receive over five hundred inches of snow annually. By late spring, temperatures warm up in the lower elevations, while the mountain snowpack begins to melt. The high mountain roads and trails are not normally free of snow until mid- to late June. Summer brings warm temperatures to most areas with hot temperatures in the valleys. Afternoon thunderstorms become common by June and can be expected into September.

General Safety

Mountain climbing is inherently dangerous. This guidebook cannot alert you to every hazard or anticipate the limitations, skill, or experience of every reader. When you choose to climb and follow any of these routes, you assume responsibility for your own safety. Before launching from any trailhead, an assessment should be made of road, trail, route, weather, and current conditions. Risks should be assessed frequently and regularly during any outing.

Mountain Safety

LIGHTNING

Being struck by lightning is a very real hazard in the state of Utah and in the Wasatch Mountains. Lightning is Utah's number one weather-related killer. Fifty-seven individuals have been killed by lightning in Utah since 1950, according to the National Weather Service. The majority of lightning deaths occur during the months of July, August, and September. It goes without saying that you should flee from summits or ridges whenever thunder is heard in the distance. Lightning can also occur when there aren't any distant signs of an electrical storm approaching. If a party is caught high on a peak during a thunderstorm, the best tactic is to move off the ridge as far as possible and to squat on packs or other insulators. Do not take shelter under talus or in a rock crevice. Electrical currents tend to go through these places. It is better to keep as low as possible on the surface, crouching on the balls of your feet. Those of us who experience an electrical storm will witness blinding flashes of light with eardrum-breaking thunder and buzzing in the air. A few have been lucky enough to survive lightning strikes. Sane people choose to avoid lightning.

HYPOTHERMIA

An afternoon thunderstorm can drop temperatures forty or more degrees at higher altitudes, and windy conditions can intensify the cold. Death can occur when a tired hiker gets caught in a storm unprepared. Hypothermia victims will have trouble keeping warm, become weak and irritable, and start to shiver uncontrollably. Anyone who starts to exhibit these signs should get to a windproof shelter. Wet clothes should be removed and warm drinks ingested if possible. The body's core temperature must be raised for survival.

ROCKFALL

Rockfall by natural means is fairly rare in the Wasatch Mountains. A recent rainstorm or the melting and freezing of snow or ice can increase the danger of rockfall. The most common type of rockfall is produced by you or other climbers. Several of the peaks see a lot of foot traffic. Caution should be taken to avoid the fall line of other parties and a helmet is advisable on some routes. Shout out "Rock!" when you launch a bomb, and take cover when you hear this signal from others.

ALTITUDE SICKNESS

The highest Wasatch peaks range between 11,000 and 11,928 feet. The thinner air at higher altitude can do strange things to people and affects everyone differently. Some people feel little effect of higher altitude, while others are affected at altitudes as low as 8,000 feet.

The most common ailment is Acute Mountain Sickness (AMS). Symptoms include headache, lack of appetite, nausea, and poor or no sleep. Anyone with these symptoms should move to lower elevations quickly. This illness can usually be prevented by gaining altitude slowly (acclimation) and drinking plenty of fluids.

WATER

Giardia lamblia is present in the lakes and streams of the Wasatch Mountains. It is an intestinal parasite that causes giardiasis, which brings with it the possibility of diarrhea, flatulence, nausea, abdominal cramps, and excessive fatigue. These symptoms last about a week, with an incubation period of one to four weeks. All water should be treated or filtered in the Wasatch Mountains.

AVALANCHES

Routes in this book radically increase in difficulty for a winter attempt and should only be considered by the most experienced climbers. Backcountry skiing, snowboarding, and snowshoeing are popular Utah pastimes. Those seeking fresh snow routinely skip crowded ski resorts and instead hike up mountains with their skis, boards, and shoes. The resorts offer an element of safety and will often use explosives to set off small, controlled slides to control avalanche conditions. In choosing to travel backcountry, climbers must diligently assess conditions, consider risks, and travel accordingly. Ninety percent of all avalanche accidents are human triggered, making them the only natural hazards caused by their victims. Slides typically kill about four people a year in Utah. Since 1985, fifty-nine people have been killed in Utah avalanches, ranking the state as the third-deadliest behind Colorado and Alaska, according to the Colorado Avalanche Information Center.

In Utah, avalanches are most common on north-facing slopes during the winter and south-facing slopes in the spring. However, avalanches may occur on ANY slope at any time. To avoid avalanches, experts recommend you:

Avalanche debris on North Peak

- Find a safe route. Traveling on ridge tops may be safest. Windward slopes may be safer than leeward slopes.
- Be aware of conditions. They can change quickly. Call the Avalanche Forecast Center ahead of time.
- Carry emergency gear and know how to use it.
- Never travel alone.

Class Ratings

The Yosemite Decimal System (YDS) has been used to rate the difficulty of the terrain described in this book. Though this system is not perfect, its wide acceptance among mountaineers and climbers makes it a logical choice. Several routes in this book have previously been rated using YDS. Since ratings are given by humans and not computers, human bias may enter into the rating. Generally, the rating is an accepted measure rendered by the consensus of the majority of climbers. A general description of the ratings is described.

Class 1 is walking. The hike to Cecret Lake, the road up Peruvian Gulch, and Gad Valley fall into this category.

Devil's Castle from the Sugarloaf/Devil's Castle saddle

Class 2 is best described as difficult cross-country travel. In the Wasatch this is usually talus hopping which may require the occasional use of hands for balance. Hikers not accustomed to Class 2 terrain may soon become tired. Many approaches in this book are Class 2, including Upper Broads Fork and Mount Superior's upper slopes.

Class 3 is where the climbing begins. Hands and feet are used not just for balance, but sometimes to hang onto the rock. Steep or large talus can be rated Class 3. Class 3 is more common on steep faces or ridges. The uninitiated may feel uncomfortable, but the holds are large and easy to locate. Several routes in this book, including the Pfeifferhorn, Sunrise, and Dromedary, are rated Class 3.

Class 4 is climbing on steep rock with smaller holds and lots of exposure. Exposure is a euphemism for the amount of "air" beneath your feet. Ropes and belays are sometimes used for safety. Falls in Class 4 terrain are usually fatal. The final summit blocks of Lone Peak, as well as Red Baldy's northeast ridge, are Class 4.

Class 5 spans a wide range of difficulty and is divided into smaller decimalized ratings (i.e., 5.1, 5.2, etc.). There are no sustained Class 5 routes in this book. However, some routes require an occasional Class 5 move. Class 5 terrain is vertical or near vertical, and ropes are usually required for safety. Falls are usually fatal.

Leave No Trace

You, the user of wilderness resources, are responsible to help protect them from environmental damage. A single footprint in fragile, alpine tundra may cause irreparable damage or damage that takes a hundred years to recover. Please tread lightly. Stay on trails, and where trails do not exist, travel on durable surfaces such as rock.

Leave No Trace, a national nonprofit organization dedicated to educating people about responsible use of the outdoors, recommends a few simple techniques for minimum-impact travel in fragile alpine zones. Their seven tenets are:

- Plan ahead and prepare
- Travel and camp on durable surfaces
- Dispose of waste properly
- Leave what you find
- Minimize campfire impacts

Lake Blanche and Sundial Peak

- Respect wildlife
- Be considerate of other visitors

For more information, you may contact Leave No Trace at www.int. org or call 800-332-4100.

The Ten Essentials

The Mountaineers, a Seattle-based hiking, climbing, and conservation group came up with a list of ten essential items that no hiker should be without. They are:

- A map and knowledge of how to use it
- A compass
- Water and a means to purify water
- Extra food
- Fire starter and matches
- A First Aid kit
- A knife or multipurpose tool
- A flashlight, headlamp, and extra batteries
- Sunscreen and sunglasses
- Extra clothing including raingear

About This Book

Never lose your spirit of exploration and your quest for adventure. The Wasatch Mountains provide an excellent environment in which one can wander and explore the unknown. Keeping that in mind, this is a mountain-climbing guidebook specifically written for climbers and peakbaggers. This guidebook intentionally does not include every route for every peak. It does include the main trailhead accesses, approaches, and routes for every peak. Some of the peaks share the same trailheads and approaches, and many of the peaks can be combined to begin and end at the same trailhead. Some peaks can be combined with the assistance of a car shuttle. Each of the five groups of peaks in this book has a similar format. Overview maps of major roads providing access to each group are included at the beginning of each group's chapter. Each group of peaks has a topographical overview map of trailheads. Finally, each peak has a detailed route map. A *route* in this book begins as the point where a visible trail ends and cross-country travel begins. The topographical maps make this distinction. *Approaches* are trails and appear as solid lines on the maps. *Routes* are dashed lines on the maps. Some peaks have visible and well-maintained trails all the way to the summit. For these peaks there is no approach, only routes. The text for the route will include information from the trailhead to the summit. Mileage figures are roundtrip and noted with the abbreviation *RT*. Elevation figures are total elevation gained. On routes where elevation loss is relevant or significant, loss figures are also included.

All roads listed as highways are Utah State Highways. Interstates are designated by the letter "I" (e.g., I-15 is Interstate 15). 4wd and 2wd are four-wheel-drive and two-wheel-drive, respectively.

Mount Timpanogos Mileage

Included in this book and the Timpanogos section are the standard mileages for Timpooneke (18 miles RT) and Aspen Grove (16 miles RT). The standard mileages have been verified by Forest Service and Park Service employees through the use of pedometers, GPS, topographical maps, and software.

I have hiked Mount Timpanogos many times through the years, and have spoken with numerous individuals who have done likewise, including one local who has climbed Timpanogos over 300 times. I have used all of the tools mentioned above, and combined those with a miles-per-hour calculation. I do not agree with the generally accepted mileage figures, and strongly believe that both Timpooneke and Aspen Grove mileages would more accurately be placed at closer to 14 miles RT.

Maps and Technology

The proliferation of Global Positioning Systems (GPS) has added a dynamic to hiking and mountaineering in recent years. A GPS system can be a wonderful addition to a standard map-and-compass style of navigation. It should not serve as the only source of navigation.

TABLE 2. *USGS Maps*

PEAK	MAPS
Twin Peaks	Dromedary
Sunrise Peak	Dromedary
Dromedary	Dromedary
Mount Superior	Dromedary
Lone Peak	Draper
South Thunder	Dromedary
North Thunder	Dromedary
Pfeifferhorn	Dromedary
White Baldy	Dromedary
Red Baldy	Dromedary
American Fork Twin	Dromedary
Mount Baldy	Dromedary
Sugarloaf Mountain	Brighton
Box Elder Peak	Timpanogos
Provo Peak	Springville
	Bridal Veil
North Peak	Nebo Basin
	Mona
Mount Nebo	Nebo Basin
	Mona

GPS coordinates were intentionally not included in this book. Although coordinates would be helpful on certain routes, they undermine the true spirit of adventure.

Ten United States Geological Survey (USGS) maps cover the peaks in this book. The maps are 7.5 minute 1:24,000 scale maps.

Estimated Hiking Times

Estimated hiking times are certainly individual in nature and unique only to you. There is no formula for determining how long each hike will take you to complete. In general, trail hiking will be different than off-trail hiking. For trail hiking, beginners will hike at a pace of 1 to 1.5 miles per hour. A moderate hiking pace is 1.5 to 2.5 miles per hour. Strong hikers will move at a pace greater than 2.5 miles per hour. Off-trail hiking times vary tremendously. Only you are qualified to estimate your hiking time.

About Corner Canyon

The Corner Canyon area of Draper City changes almost daily. It is at the crux of the struggle between urban development and protecting access to public lands and wilderness areas. Corner Canyon provides western and southern approaches to the Lone Peak Wilderness area, and access to it is constantly being threatened.

In a typical year the gate at the beginning of Corner Canyon Road is open or closed depending on the season. The year 2005, however, was far from typical. The gate opened in mid-winter, but closed mid-spring and will remain closed indefinitely. One of the more popular trailheads to Lone Peak, Jacobs Ladder, is currently not accessible by automobile. It is still available for bikes, motorcycles, and ATVs. Currently, private negotiations are taking place regarding land acquisition in and around the Corner Canyon area. The primary issue at hand is determining who owns the land and how to mitigate the impact of erosion. Since the negotiations are private, the information is confidential.

Recent road construction has paved 2000 East and made the road a continuation of Wasatch Boulevard. The result has been a new turn being required to access Corner Canyon Road and a new area being developed around Corner Canyon gate. Draper City owns the land at the gate to Corner Canyon. The city is committed to developing a trailhead and park at the gate. The newly signed trailhead has been named Orson Smith Trailhead. Future plans call for a park in addition to the new signage. Given the new trailhead's proximity to a major road like Wasatch Boulevard, some new challenges will be presented. The new signage has already been a victim of vandals. The future remains uncertain for this area.

About the Town of Alpine

Southern access to the Lone Peak Wilderness area faces challenges similar to those of the Corner Canyon area of Draper. In fact, the line between the towns of Draper and Alpine diminishes with the pressure of urban development. The development of Draper City continues to push south and east over the Traverse Mountains while the town of Alpine continues to push to the north and west toward the Traverse Mountains. A new road has been constructed which connects Utah State Highway 92 to Draper City. The road travels up and over the Traverse Mountains and descends into Draper City and the Salt Lake Valley.

The town of Alpine has become a popular and desirable place for many to live. In recent years the increased popularity has left the town of Alpine with challenges regarding urban development and proper use of open space. Urban development continues to creep up the mountain toward Lone Peak Wilderness. Private land ownership already has and will continue to modify access points for the southern end of Lone Peak Wilderness. Schoolhouse Springs currently is the access point, but it is surrounded by the pressures of private land ownership and development. The future of this trailhead is uncertain.

I

Twin Peaks Group

Introduction

Twin Peaks Wilderness forms a part of the dramatic backdrop seen on the east side of the Salt Lake Valley southeast of Salt Lake City. Highway 190 follows Big Cottonwood Creek along the northern boundary and separates this wilderness from Mount Olympus Wilderness to the north. Highway 210 follows Little Cottonwood Creek along the southern boundary and stands between Twin Peaks Wilderness and Lone Peak Wilderness to the south.

Twin Peaks Wilderness Group offers five peaks and two classic traverses. The easiest route on any of the peaks is Class 3. Twin Peaks is the most popular peak as well as the most difficult. Mount Superior and Monte Cristo to the east offer the easiest approach. The Cottonwood Traverse is one of the classic traverses in the Wasatch, but is less frequented than the Lone Peak Wilderness traverses to the south.

The Twin Peaks Wilderness from the north

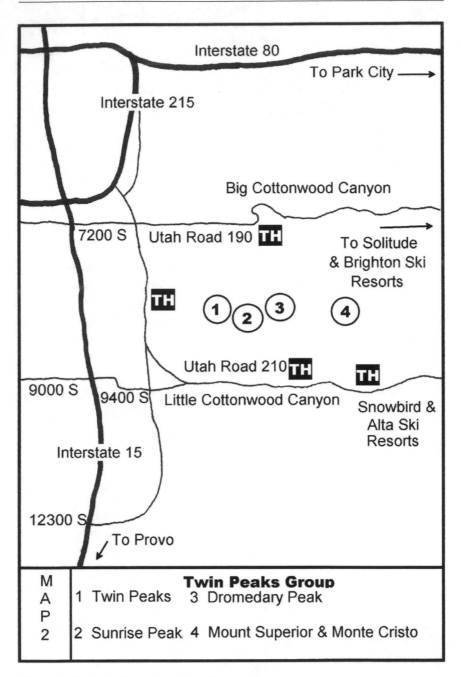

MAP 2. *Twin Peaks Group Road Overview*

1. Broads Fork Twin Peaks – 11,330 feet & 11,328 feet

See maps on pages 16 and 19

Twin Peaks is the crown jewel of the Twin Peaks Wilderness area. Although not the highest set of twin peaks in the Wasatch, Broads Fork Twin Peaks play second to none. They are a prominent part of the Salt Lake City skyline and are impressive when viewed from any direction. They can be approached from several canyons and drainages, but are mainly approached via Broads Fork.

TRAILHEADS

■ Broads Fork Trailhead

At 6,200 feet, this trailhead provides access to the most common approach for Twin Peaks, Sunrise, and Dromedary. Southeast of Salt Lake City, exit I-215 at 6200 South (Exit 6). Turn east toward the mountains and continue 1.6 miles to the mouth of Big Cottonwood Canyon. Signs for Brighton and Solitude Ski Resorts will point the way. Begin measuring from the intersection with Wasatch Boulevard at the mouth of the canyon. Drive east up the canyon and pass Storm Mountain picnic area after 2.8 miles. Continue east past several private homes and reach Mill B South trailhead after 4.2 miles. The trailhead is on the south side of the road as the road makes a sharp "S" turn. The trail to Lake Blanche leaves from the east side of the parking lot. Broads Fork trailhead leaves from the west end of the lot. Overflow parking is available along the highway.

■ Deaf Smith Canyon Trailhead

This trailhead at 5,200 feet provides access to Twin Peaks north ridge route via a western approach. Private property currently blocks easy access into the canyon with a private driveway at the beginning of the trail. Parking is limited in the Golden Hills subdivision. Southeast of Salt Lake City, exit I-215 at 6200 South (Exit 6). Turn east toward the mountains and continue 1.6 miles to the mouth of Big Cottonwood Canyon. Go straight (south) through the intersection (7200 South) and reach Kings Hill Drive (8345 South) after 3.1 miles. Turn left (east) onto Kings Hill Drive and continue 0.4 miles to Golden

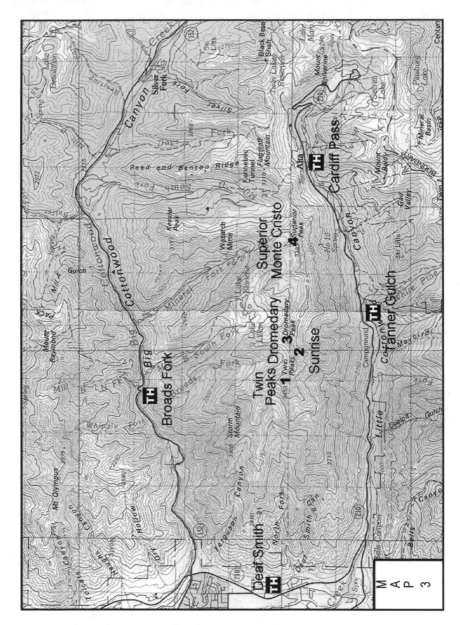

MAP 3. *Twin Peaks Group Trailhead Overview*

Oaks Drive (8620 South). Turn left and park after 3.6 miles. A chained gate at the top of Golden Oaks Drive marks the beginning of the unmarked trailhead.

APPROACHES

■ Broads Fork

This is the most common approach to Twin Peaks, Sunrise, and Dromedary. From the west end of the Mill B South trailhead parking lot, a sign marks the beginning of the Broads Fork trail. Begin by climbing west and enter the Twin Peaks Wilderness area after 0.2 miles. Climb west into Broads Fork drainage approaching the stream. Short of the stream, turn left (south) and climb steeply to a stream crossing. A sturdy, wooden bridge crosses the stream at 7,500 feet and 1.2 miles from the trailhead. Cross the bridge and climb past several small benches another 1.0 miles to reach the meadows at 8,400 feet. The trail is well maintained and clearly distinct to the meadows. A small spur trail branches to the right to reach the top of a knoll and provides access to the north ridge route. The main trail continues straight (east) across the meadows toward the stream. Consolidated snow during springtime makes it possible to travel directly up the drainage from the meadows. In the absence of snow, cross the stream and continue on a less-distinct trail south. Both routes converge higher in the Broads Fork drainage. Caution should be taken above the meadows during spring climbs. Several of the slopes are prone to avalanches, and ice axe and crampons are recommended during spring ascents. Continue up the drainage and climb beneath the north face of Sunrise Peak to 9,800 feet. Beneath the shadow of Sunrise's north face, the southeast route to Twin Peaks turns right (west). The east route to Dromedary goes left (east). The west ridge of Dromedary and the east ridge of Sunrise are straight ahead.

■ Deaf Smith Canyon

Deaf Smith Canyon provides a western approach to Twin Peaks. If your objective is Twin Peaks, Sunrise, and Dromedary, you are better off choosing Broads Fork approach or Tanners Gulch route (see Route 2.1 on page 22). Twin Peaks via this approach is usually enough for one day. From your parking area in the Golden Hills subdivision, pass through the chained gate and turn right. Continue southeast for 0.2 miles on a well-defined trail to reach a residential driveway at the canyon's entrance. Walk up the residential driveway a short distance to a dirt path east of a house. Begin climbing on the south side of the stream a short distance before crossing to the north side. Stay on the north side of the stream until 5,800 feet as the canyon narrows. Cross to the south side of the stream and climb 100 feet. The canyon opens a bit to the north as cliffs block easy passage to the east. Cross the creek at 5,900 feet and pass a small cliffband on the north side of the stream. The canyon narrows to a few feet and passage may be difficult during high run-off periods in spring and early summer. Continue on the north side of the stream to 6,900 feet where the canyon opens up again. Cross to the south side of the stream and begin climbing steeply to reach a meadow area at 7,900 feet after 3.0 miles. Continue climbing straight (east) across the meadow and reach a burn area from a wildfire years ago. The canyon splits at the meadow. Twin Peaks can be reached by taking the right (south) fork and traveling cross-country to reach the western ridge of Twin Peaks. Stay left (north) to begin Route 1.3 into upper Deaf Smith Canyon and the north ridge.

ROUTES

■ **1.1 Southeast Ridge, Class 3–4**

From Broads Fork Trailhead: 9.0 miles RT; 5,130 feet

From 9,800 feet in upper Broads Fork, contour right (west) and continue climbing to the Sunrise/Twin Peaks saddle. The final 100 feet to the saddle can be tricky. Early season climbs can present a 45-degree, snow-covered ascent and the ridge may be corniced. During the summer this is a steep, loose scree slope through a broken cliff band. Aim for the left (south) side of the saddle and reach it at 10,780 feet. From the 10,780-foot saddle, scramble along the ridge a few hundred feet over solid blocks. The climbing begins. You may contour northwest toward the most prominent and visible scree gully. This route is Class 3 but not recommended since it receives rock

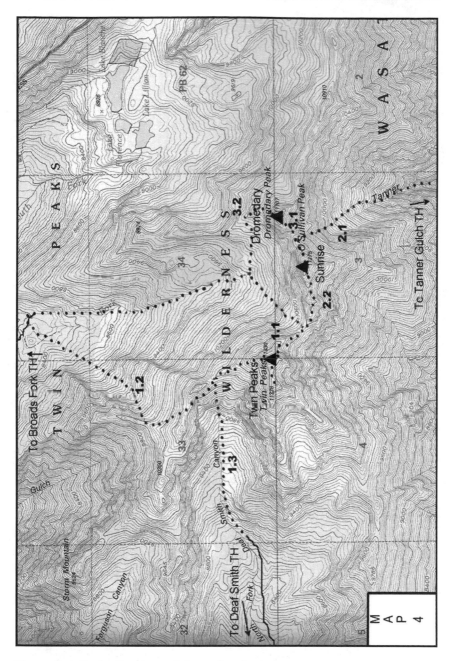

Map 4. *Twin Peaks, Sunrise, and Dromedary Routes*

fall from most of the upper route. The standard route climbs slightly and follows broken ledges to arrive at the base of a 30-foot chimney-and-crack system. Most of the route to this point is Class 3. Climb the 30-foot chimney which requires some Class 4 moves. From the top of the chimney scramble a few more feet to the base of the final summit cone. A climber's trail switchbacks the final feet to the east (highest) summit of Twin Peaks at 11,330 feet. The west summit of Twin Peaks can be reached via a short Class 3 scramble staying on the ridge the entire traverse.

▪ 1.2 North Ridge Robinson Variation, Class 3

From Broads Fork Trailhead: 8.0 miles RT; 5,130 feet

The north ridge can be reached by using the Broads Fork approach for the first 2.2 miles to the meadow at 8,400 feet. From the meadow the trail continues toward the creek on the left (east) side of the drainage. A few yards before the stream, look for a trail branching to the right. Take this trail and contour around the knoll in the meadow to the south and then to the west. Follow a faint trail and cairns through sporadic willows and boulders (snow in early season) to reach the prominent, east-facing couloir. Enter the couloir and begin ascending Class 2 terrain steeply to the ridge. Gain the ridge at 10,000 feet and peek down into Salt Lake Valley. From the top of the couloir, turn left (south) and contour along the left (east) side of the ridge. Reach a small notch where upper Deaf Smith Canyon comes into view and the entire north face of Twin Peaks is visible. Class 3 scrambling begins as the ridge turns slightly east and south toward Twin Peak's east summit. The traverse gains little elevation to this point. Route 1.3 ascending from upper Deaf Smith Canyon joins the ridge here. The difficulty eases to Class 2 at the base of the final ascent to Twin's east summit. It is best to stay on the east side of this ridge for the final ascent to Twin Peak's summit.

▪ 1.3 West via Upper Deaf Smith Canyon, Class 3

From Deaf Smith Canyon Trailhead: 9.0 miles RT; 6,130 feet

From the meadow at 7,900 feet in upper Deaf Smith Canyon, continue climbing toward the east staying near the low point in the drainage. The trail is faint to nonexistent above the meadow. Watch for sporadic cairns staying near the stream. Climb straight east above the trees to 9,000 feet. The trees become sporadic and the terrain transitions to boulders or consolidated snow in early season. Climb boulders or consolidated snow east staying near the middle of the drainage. Reach a cliff band at 9,900 feet. Class 3 climbing is required to negotiate the middle of the cliff band. Continue straight east toward the ridge and reach it at 10,500 feet after 4.2 miles. Share the final few hundred feet with Route 1.2. Turn right (south) toward Twin Peaks and continue along the ridge toward the summit. The left (east) side of the ridge is generally easier and the final ascent is Class 2 terrain.

2. Sunrise Peak – 11,275 feet

See maps on pages 16 and 19

Sunrise Peak is the mountaineer's name given to this 11,275-foot peak. Some topographical maps have named the peak O'Sullivan. Whatever you decide to call it, it is a peak worthy of attention. Most overlook Sunrise Peak in search of Twin Peaks' loftier and more

Sunrise Peak from the north

popular summit. Their loss is your gain as you're more likely to find solitude on the large, rounded summit. The view down Sunrise's north face will impress you.

TRAILHEADS

■ **Broads Fork**

See page 15 for description

■ **Tanners Gulch Trailhead**

This trailhead at 7,200 feet provides access to Sunrise's east route and Dromedary's west route. If approaching from the north exit I-215 at 6200 South (Exit 6). Turn east toward the mountains and continue 1.6 miles to the mouth of Big Cottonwood Canyon. Go straight (south) through the intersection following signs for Alta and Snowbird Ski Resorts. Reach the electric notification sign at the mouth of Little Cottonwood Canyon after 5.4 miles.

If approaching from the south exit, I-15 at 9000 South (Exit 295). Drive east 6.0 miles to Wasatch Boulevard. Continue straight (east) and reach the electric notification sign at the mouth of Little Cottonwood Canyon after 7.2 miles. Measuring from this point, continue east past the popular rock-climbing areas in lower Little Cottonwood Canyon and pass the power plant at 1.8 miles. Tanners Flat Campground is on the right side of the road after 4.3 miles. The trail leaves from the Tanners Flat Avalanche sign on the west side of the road. Tanners Gulch looms ominously to the north.

APPROACH

■ **Broads Fork**

See page 17 for description

ROUTES

■ **2.1 Tanners Gulch, Class 3**

From Tanners Gulch Trailhead: 3.6 miles RT; 4,075 feet

Tanners Gulch

This makes a great early spring snow climb. Wet-slide avalanche conditions should be assessed before committing to this route. A helmet is mandatory due to rock fall dangers. Free of snow Tanners Gulch is still a viable option as the climbing is primarily Class 3 in difficulty. Leave the highway from the Tanners Flat Avalanche Area sign and begin hiking west through the trees on a faint trail. Gain 100 feet before dropping into Tanners Gulch after 0.2 miles. Begin climbing along the bottom of the drainage. The cliffs on both the east and west sides soon close in. Climb past several small cliff bands and possible waterfalls. Tanners Gulch splits at 8,500 feet after 0.5 miles. The left (west) fork continues the most direct route to the Sunrise/ Dromedary saddle, but is blocked by a cliff band in the absence of snow. The right (east) fork can be more easily ascended bypassing the cliff band later in the season. With snow, ascend the left fork to 9,500 feet. Without snow, ascend the right fork a short distance to about 8,800 feet. Tanners Gulch opens up at this point. Climb left (west) out of the gully and begin an ascending traverse to the north-west. Your goal is to get to the darker colored quartzite rock at 9,500 feet. This point marks the entry into the final couloir leading to the Dromedary/Sunrise saddle. Cross snow or open tundra and boulders to 9,500 feet, then climb steeply for 900 feet to 10,400 feet. A large boulder blocks easy passage further upward. Bypass the boulder on the right (east) by ascending broken ledges. The final 130 feet to the saddle are steep, loose, and can be treacherous in the absence of snow. Carefully pick your way to the Sunrise/Dromedary saddle at 10,530 feet. This saddle can also be reached by climbing 700 feet directly south from upper Broads Fork. See Broads Fork approach on page 17 for description. From the saddle, begin climbing large blocks to the west via Class 3 scrambling. Generally, it is easier to stay left (south) along the ridge to avoid the exposure of the north face. Carefully pick your way through the large blocks initially blocking your passage and stay close to the ridge when possible to avoid loose scree. The north face of Sunrise drops precipitously to your right (north). Several calculated Class 3 moves are required to gain the next 100 feet. The angle eases and transitions to Class 2–3 climbing. Continue climbing along the left (south) side of the ridge and reach the summit at 11,275 feet.

■ 2.2 West Ridge, Class 3

From Broads Fork Trailhead: 8.0 miles RT; 5,075 feet

The west ridge route uses the same Broads Fork approach (see page 17 for description) as the Twin Peaks Southeast Route 1.1. From 9,800 feet in upper Broads Fork, climb right (west) toward the 10,780-foot Sunrise/Twin Peaks saddle. Aim for the left (south) side of the saddle. From this saddle drop down and left (south) about 50 feet into Little Cottonwood Canyon. The loss in elevation will bypass Class 5 climbing from the saddle directly. Traverse left (south) around the southwest facing slopes for 30 to 40 feet. After rounding the corner, turn left (east) and begin climbing Class 3 rock. Climb 400 feet to reach an 11,100-foot point along the west ridge or contour around the south slopes to avoid unnecessary elevation gain. Pass the saddle between the 11,100-foot point and Sunrise's true summit, then continue the ascent on Class 2 terrain a short distance to Sunrise's summit.

3. Dromedary Peak – 11,107 feet

See maps on pages 16 and 19

Dromedary's neighbor, Sunrise Peak, is often overlooked, while Dromedary Peak is ignored altogether. From Dromedary's summit you will be treated to an unobstructed view of Lake Blanche to the northeast. You may sit atop Dromedary and contemplate the Cottonwood Traverse toward Monte Cristo Peak to the east. Either way, Dromedary's summit will more than justify your effort to climb it.

TRAILHEADS

■ **Broads Fork**

See page 15 for description

■ **Tanners Gulch**

See page 22 for description

Dromedary Peak viewed from upper Broads Fork

APPROACHES

▪ **Broads Fork**

> *See page 17 for description*

▪ **Tanners Gulch**

> *See page 22 for description*

ROUTES

▪ **3.1 West Ridge, Class 3**

From Broads Fork Trailhead: 8.0 miles RT; 4,910 feet

From Tanners Gulch Trailhead: 3.6 miles RT; 3,910 feet

Climb Tanners Gulch or use the Broads Fork approach to reach the Dromedary/Sunrise saddle at 10,530 feet. Here the climbing begins. From the saddle descend south into upper Tanners Gulch for 20 to 30 feet on the Little Cottonwood Canyon side of the ridge. Do an ascending contour on a broken ledge system to the east. Round a corner as Dromedary's summit becomes visible to your right (east). Climb the most obvious gully on loose rock to gain the ridge just west of the summit. Scramble along the ridge a short distance to the summit on mostly Class 3 rock.

▪ **3.2 East Ridge, Class 3**

From Broads Fork Trailhead: 8.0 miles RT; 4,910 feet

Use the Broads Fork approach to reach 9,800 feet. From 9,800 feet in upper Broads Fork, turn left (east) and aim for the northeast shoulder of Dromedary. Climb under the north face of Dromedary to reach the east ridge. Climb loose scree and boulders or snow to reach the ridge between Broads Fork and Blanche Fork at 10,400 feet. The view down to Lake Blanche is spectacular. From the Lake Blanche/Broads Fork ridge, climb right (south) staying near the ridge. Climb a short, steep section to reach the east-facing slopes. The remainder of the route is visible from this point. Climb broken ledges on gentle, sloping rock. Care should be taken to stay left (south) along the east slope

Left to Right: *Dromedary, Sunrise, and Twin Peaks*

to avoid the exposure of the north face. The ridge along the north is more difficult. Climb a few hundred feet along Class 3 rock to reach the summit at 11,107 feet.

■ The Triple Traverse, Class 4

From Broads Fork Trailhead: 10.0 miles RT; 6,200 feet

From Tanners Gulch Trailhead: 5.2 miles RT; 5,700 feet

This traverse is often referred to as Tanners Traverse. Twin Peaks, Sunrise, and Dromedary can be climbed in one long day from either Tanners Gulch or Broads Fork.

From Broads Fork climb Twin Peaks via the southeast ridge. Descend the southeast ridge and return to the Twin Peaks/Sunrise saddle at 10,780 feet. Follow the west ridge route of Sunrise to its summit. Descend the east ridge of Sunrise to reach the Sunrise/ Dromedary saddle at 10,530 feet. Descend slightly and climb the west ridge route to reach Dromedary's summit. Descend Dromedary's east slope and return to upper Broads Fork. The traverse can be completed in either direction.

From Tanners Gulch climb Dromedary's west ridge to Dromedary's summit. Retrace your steps and return to the Dromedary/

Sunrise saddle. Climb Sunrise's east ridge, stand atop its summit, then descend its west ridge to the Twin Peaks/Sunrise saddle. Climb Twin Peaks southeast route. Rest on the summit and return down Twin Peaks' southeast route, up Sunrise's west ridge, and descend Sunrise's east ridge to your return down Tanners Gulch.

4. Mount Superior and Monte Cristo – 11,040 feet & 11,132 feet

See map on page 29

Mount Superior and Monte Cristo stand tall, providing a scenic backdrop for those who ski the slopes of Alta and Snowbird Ski Resorts. Joined by a short ridge, the two peaks are inseparable. Most climb the two together. The cliffs west of Monte Cristo block easy passage farther along the ridge and have intimidated even the most seasoned climbers. Superior and Monte Cristo are a worthy objective in any season.

TRAILHEAD

■ **Cardiff Pass**

This trailhead is at 8,640 feet. If approaching from the north, exit I-215 at 6200 South (Exit 6). Turn east toward the mountains and

Superior and Monte Cristo from upper Blanche Fork

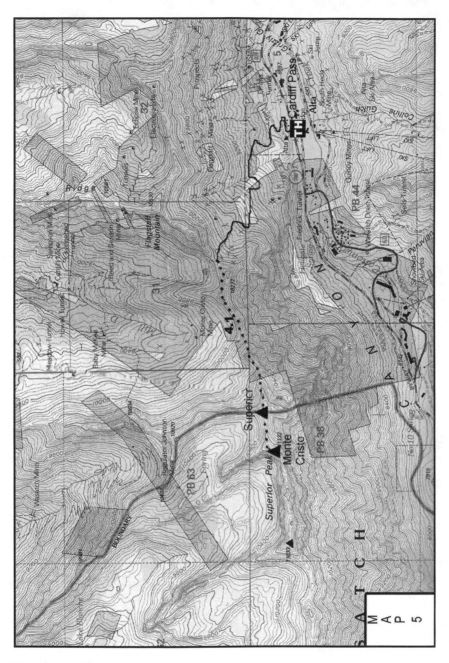

MAP 5. *Monte Cristo and Superior Route*

continue 1.6 miles to the mouth of Big Cottonwood Canyon. Go straight (south) through the intersection, following signs for Alta and Snowbird Ski Resorts. Reach the electric notification sign at the mouth of Little Cottonwood Canyon after 5.4 miles.

If approaching from the south, exit I-15 at 9000 South (Exit 295). Turn east and continue 6.0 miles to Wasatch Boulevard. Continue straight (east) and reach the electric notification sign at the mouth of Little Cottonwood Canyon after 7.2 miles. Measuring from this point, continue east past the popular rock-climbing areas in lower Little Cottonwood Canyon and pass the power plant after 1.8 miles. The Tanners Flat Campground is reached after 4.2 miles. Continue east past White Pine trailhead at 5.2 miles, pass all four entries to Snowbird Ski Resort, and reach a parking area just east of the Alta Fire Station after 8.0 miles. There is ample parking on both sides of the road.

APPROACH

▪ Cardiff Pass

From the parking area walk down the paved road 0.1 miles to a road directly west of the Alta Fire Station. Turn right (north) and begin hiking north and east up the paved road. This trailhead is not marked and climbs through private property for the first 0.2 miles. The road makes two switchbacks. After the second switchback, look for a trail leaving the pavement to the north. Clear of the houses and private property, continue climbing west. The old mining road forks after 0.4 miles. Go left (west) up a now single-track trail that continues climbing west. The right fork continues up to the old Flagstaff mine to the north. Climb steeply and make one switchback to reach a small, flat area. Continue climbing steeply north to reach Cardiff Pass at 10,000 feet.

ROUTE

▪ 4.1 East Ridge, Class 3

From Cardiff Pass Trailhead: 5.0 miles RT; 2,600 feet

From Cardiff Pass turn left (west) and contour past two minor summits along the ridge. The route begins by staying on the right (north) side of the ridge past Point 10,277. Cross to the left (south) side and bypass the other minor summit, staying on the left (south) side of the ridge for the remainder of the route. Contour 0.3 miles along the ridge gaining little elevation. The climbing begins. Ascend loose scree slightly left (south) of the ridge crest. Much of the initial ascent is Class 2. Reach a small southeast ridge at 10,450 feet and continue an ascending traverse along the east slopes. Continue ascending, drawing closer to the ridge. The final 400 feet of scrambling to the summit is Class 3 with some exposure along the ridge.

The summit of Monte Cristo is 0.2 miles to the west along the ridge. Continue along the ridge, losing 100 feet elevation initially. Continue Class 2 hiking to the west and reach a small, grassy gully northeast of Monte Cristo. Hike up the gentle gully to reach a notch 60 feet below Monte Cristo's summit. It is Class 3 climbing for the final 60 feet to the summit of Monte Cristo at 11,132 feet. Peek down the southwest slope to whet your appetite for the most difficult traverse in the Wasatch.

The Cottonwood Traverse, Class 4, Class 5.0–5.2

From Cardiff Pass Trailhead & Broads Fork Exit: 8.5 miles total, 3,700 feet gain, 6,050 feet loss

A car shuttle is required for this traverse. It is a difficult 2.1-mile traverse and technically the most difficult traverse in this book. The approach is relatively short via Cardiff Pass, but the crux of the route descending west from Monte Cristo deters many people. Engage the traverse by descending a few feet south from Monte Cristo's summit toward a now visible southwest-facing chute. Climb down the chute in Class 3 terrain 70 feet until it is possible to contour right (west) to gain the ridge. A small clump of trees will mark your access point to the ridge. Gain the ridge to engage the crux of the traverse. This section of the ridge is knife-edge and exposed on both sides. Staying on the ridge requires low Class 5 moves to down-climb 80 feet. Past the crux, scramble along the ridge a short distance in Class 3 terrain to

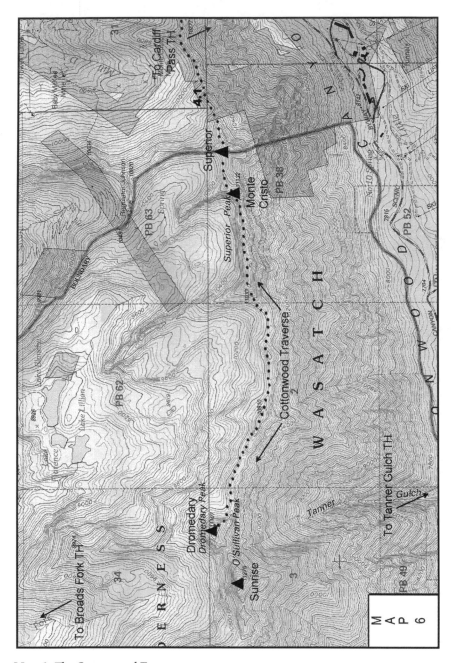

MAP 6. *The Cottonwood Traverse*

The Cottonwood Traverse from the southeast

reach a low point at 10,800 feet after 0.2 miles. Gain 200 feet in the next 0.1 miles. Lose 100 feet before climbing to Unnamed Point 11,033 after 0.5 miles. Unnamed Point 11,033 is the point of the ridge running south from Lake Blanche and offers an exit point. From Unnamed Point 11,033 lose 350 feet in the next 0.3 miles on loose, rocky terrain. Scramble 0.2 miles and gain a highpoint along the ridge at 10,800 feet after 1.0 miles. Lose 150 feet, then resume climbing to Unnamed Point 10,910 after 1.4 miles. Lose 150 feet in the next 0.2 miles and continue a fairly level traverse toward Dromedary's southeast shoulder. Reach Dromedary's southeast shoulder at 10,700 feet after 1.9 miles. Climb steeply a short distance in mixed Class 3 and Class 4 terrain to reach Dromedary's summit after 2.1 miles. It is possible to contour onto the gentler east slabs of Dromedary to ascend to the summit. Descend either the northeast ridge or east slabs of Dromedary and exit via Broads Fork.

2

Lone Peak Group

Introduction

The Lone Peak Wilderness is the largest of a trio of wilderness areas just southeast of Salt Lake City. Highway 92 follows American Fork Canyon. Coupled with a short stretch of Highway 144, it forms the southern-southeastern boundary of the Wilderness. This wilderness shares its southern border with Timpanogos Cave National Monument. Highway 210 along Little Cottonwood Creek forms the northern boundary and separates Lone Peak Wilderness from the Twin Peaks Wilderness.

Difficult, remote, and rugged describe the peaks in the Lone Peak Wilderness Group. They are, as a group, the most difficult in this book. The Lone Peak Group contains six peaks and two unique traverses. Five of the peaks sit along the ridge crest beginning a mile west of Snowbird and ending at Lone Peak southeast of Salt Lake City. The Lone Peak Group offers long approaches, substantial elevation gain, and limited access points. Climbing any peak in the Lone Peak Group will leave you wanting to climb more. Each peak is unique and offers an experience for those willing to commit to them.

5. Lone Peak – 11,253 feet

See maps on pages 38 and 44

Lone Peak is an attractive peak for a variety of reasons. Its prominence on the Salt Lake City skyline tempts many who can see the jagged summit from the valley floor. Easy trailhead access only tempts more. Its beautiful, glacial cirque alone is a worthy destination. Lone Peak can be approached from at least a half dozen trailheads. Those

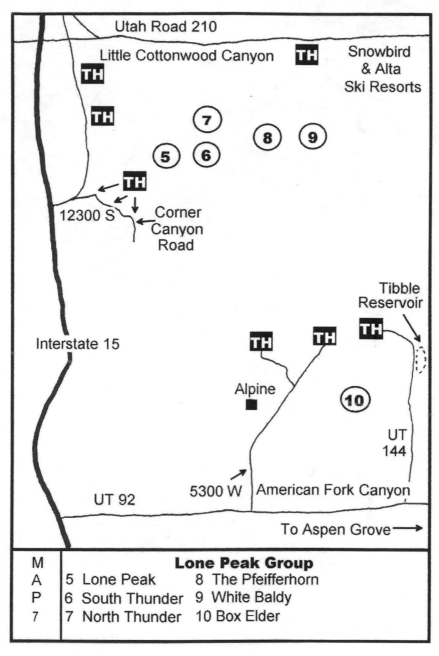

Utah Road 210

Little Cottonwood Canyon **TH** Snowbird & Alta Ski Resorts

TH

TH

⑦

⑧ ⑨

⑤ ⑥

TH

12300 S Corner Canyon Road

Tibble Reservoir

Interstate 15

TH **TH**

TH

Alpine

⑩

UT 144

5300 W | American Fork Canyon

UT 92

To Aspen Grove ⟶

M A P 7	**Lone Peak Group**	
	5 Lone Peak	8 The Pfeifferhorn
	6 South Thunder	9 White Baldy
	7 North Thunder	10 Box Elder

MAP 7. *Lone Peak Group Road Overview*

Lone Peak viewed from the cirque to the west

who choose to climb Lone Peak from any route can expect a long approach of five to six miles with 5-6,000 feet of elevation gain.

TRAILHEADS

■ Orson Smith Park

This trailhead at 4,800 feet is the lowest trailhead in this book, located at the gate for Corner Canyon Road. Take I-15 south of Salt Lake City and take the 12300 South exit (Exit 291). Turn east and continue 1.8 miles to 1300 East. Turn right (south) and continue to the bottom of the hill to a rotary intersection on Pioneer Road (12400 South). Make a 270-degree loop around the intersection to make certain your direction of travel is now east on Pioneer Road. Reach an intersection at 2000 East after 3.0 miles. Turn right (south) and reach the turnoff for Corner Canyon Road after 3.3 miles. Turn left and park here. The trailhead is marked.

■ Draper Ridge

This unmarked trailhead is at 5,300 feet. Take I-15 south of Salt Lake City and take the 12300 South exit (Exit 291). Turn east and continue 1.8 miles to 1300 East. Turn right (south) and continue to the bottom of the hill to a rotary intersection on Pioneer Road (12400 South). Make a 270-degree loop around the intersection to make certain your direction of travel is now east on Pioneer Road. Reach an intersection at 2000 East after 3.0 miles. Turn right (south) and reach the turnoff for Corner Canyon Road after 3.3 miles. Continue along the dirt road until it begins to turn toward the east. Reach a small parking area after 5.0 miles. Parking for one or two cars is available on the right (south) side of the road. This road is passable for most passenger cars and is well maintained. Exact closing dates vary each year for the Corner Canyon gate, which is controlled by Draper City. A sign on the gate offers (801) 576-6517 as a phone number for information.

■ Jacobs Ladder

This unmarked trailhead is at 5,600 feet. Take I-15 south of Salt Lake City and take the 12300 South exit. Turn east and continue 1.8 miles to 1300 East. Turn right (south) and continue to the bottom of the hill to a rotary intersection on Pioneer Road (12400 South). Make a 270-degree loop around the intersection to make certain your direction of travel is now east on Pioneer Road. Reach an intersection at 2000 East after 3.0 miles. Turn right (south) and reach the turnoff for Corner Canyon Road after 3.3 miles. Pass the Draper Ridge trailhead after 5.0 miles. The road is passable for most passenger cars and is well maintained. Continue along the road as it begins winding east and climbs to reach the Jacobs Ladder trailhead after 5.9 miles. Parking is on the right (south) side of the road at 5,600 feet. Exact closing dates vary each year for the Corner Canyon gate, which is controlled by Draper City. A sign on the gate offers (801) 576-6517 as a phone number for information.

■ Big Willow

This trailhead is at 5,100 feet. Take I-15 south of Salt Lake City and take the 12300 South exit (Exit 291). Turn east and continue 1.8 miles to 1300 East. Continue straight through the intersection as the road winds around to the north. Reach a stoplight after 3.0 miles and the intersection with Wasatch Boulevard. Turn right at the stoplight and drive east on Wasatch Boulevard, reaching Hidden Valley Park after 5.8 miles. The trailhead for Big Willow is unmarked but leaves from the east end of the parking area on a paved path.

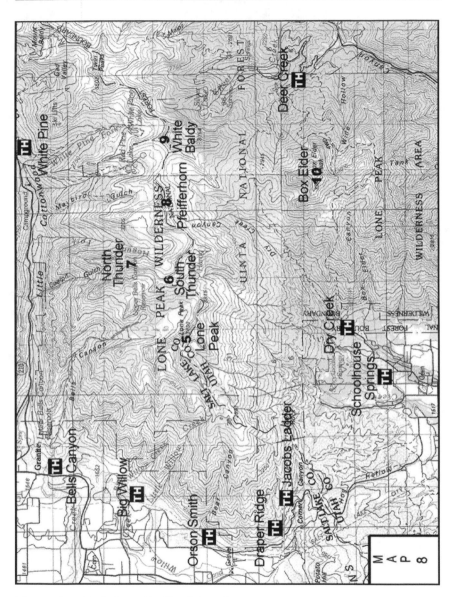

MAP 8. *Lone Peak Group Trailhead Overview*

▪ Schoolhouse Springs

This trailhead is at 5,300 feet and provides access to Lone Peak's south ridge and South Thunder's south ridge. Take Exit 284 from I-15 north of the town of Lehi and turn east onto Highway 92. Continue east toward the town of Alpine for 5.6 miles to reach a stoplight at 5300 West. Turn left (north) toward Alpine and continue for 7.4 miles to reach 200 North. Turn right (east) and go one block to a four-way intersection. Turn left (north) onto Grove Drive. After 9.3 miles reach a "T" intersection and turn left (north) onto Oakridge Drive (13440 N 4150 W). Continue on Oakridge Drive for 9.5 miles to Aspen Drive (13560 N 4300 W). Turn left onto Aspen Drive and continue to Aspen Grove and the trailhead after 9.7 miles. Turn right and park near the gate. The trailhead is unmarked and parking is limited.

APPROACHES

▪ Bear Canyon via Orson Smith

This approach is quickly gaining popularity due to challenges with the Corner Canyon gate closure. Access has been limited to Draper Ridge and Jacobs Ladder trailheads. Leave from the Orson Smith Park trailhead near the gate at Corner Canyon. Begin climbing the hill to a junction with the Bonneville Shoreline Trail (BST). From the junction with BST, a sign marks the beginning of the Cherry Canyon Logging Trail. This trail begins climbing the hillside between Bear Canyon to the left (north) and Cherry Canyon to the right (south). Climb 500 feet on a well-maintained trail as it switchbacks and crosses a small ravine at 5,700 feet. Continue climbing right (south) to an overlook into Cherry Canyon at 6,100 feet. Climb switchbacks to reach the ridge between Cherry Canyon and Bear Canyon at 7,200 feet. The angle eases as the trail climbs into upper Cherry Canyon at 7,600 feet. Climb steeply at the head of Cherry Canyon to reach a small junction at 8,400 feet. At this junction a faint trail contours slightly to the right (south) to join the Draper Ridge approach. Continue straight (east) and contour into Bear Canyon. The open slopes give way to a welcome canopy of trees and lush undergrowth. Reach a small, reliable spring, cross a creek, and begin climbing along the north side of Bear Canyon. Climb straight (east) over a small saddle and reach a meadow area which is home to the Outlaw Cabin at 9,300 feet. The cabin was constructed in 1997 and has assisted in the rescue of stranded hikers over time. It is available for public use and has seen many campers. The trail ends just north of the cabin.

■ Draper Ridge

The Draper Ridge approach has fallen out of favor in recent years for the shorter Jacobs Ladder approach. Both routes converge at 9,200 feet on the mountain. As a result, the Draper Ridge approach is severely eroded and overgrown. Leave the parking area and begin climbing steeply up a four-wheel-drive (4wd) track to the north. Climb either the gentle 4wd road as it switchbacks up the mountain or the 4wd track straight up the mountain to 6,200 feet. Look for a trail that branches off the road to the right (east) as the road continues to the north. Climb into a gully initially and onto the next ridge to the east. Continue climbing through mountain mahogany to 8,300 feet. Above 8,300 feet, appreciate the open slopes and your freedom from the steep, overgrown trail. Continue climbing straight (east) and reach the route ascending Jacobs Ladder from the right (south) at 9,200 feet.

■ Jacobs Ladder

Currently, this is the most popular approach to Lone Peak. From the parking area on the right (south) side of the road, continue walking up the road a few yards to a recently established trail on the left (north). Take the trail and climb to a 4wd road on the ridge to the north. Turn right (east) and follow the road along the spur ridge for 1.0 miles to the east. At this point the jeep road turns to a single track and begins climbing steeply through brush and scrub oak. This trail is steep and can be brutally hot in the summer. It climbs up the spur ridge known as Jacobs Ladder. The trail up Jacobs Ladder eventually joins the Draper Ridge route coming up from the left (west) at 9,200 feet.

■ Big Willow

The Big Willow approach leaves from the east end of Hidden Valley Park. Begin on a paved footpath and continue 50 yards to a sign pointing the way to the Bonneville Shoreline Trail (BST). Leave the paved trail and follow the 4wd road as it contours in a northeasterly direction. Reach a locked gate and a sign for BST after 0.2 miles . The BST cuts back to the south at the gate. Continue through the gate up the 4wd road until it turns right (east) into Big Willow Canyon. Look for a trail to your right. It is well hidden and easy to miss. If you cross the creek running under the road, you have gone too far. Find the trail and climb steeply up the west-facing slope. Climb steadily, eventually winding into Little Willow Canyon which is south of Big Willow Canyon. Turn left (east) as the angle eases and wind through huge boulders to a small junction. An avalanche warning sign marks this junction. The trail continues a few yards to an overlook in Little Willow Canyon. At the avalanche warning sign, make a sharp switchback left (north) toward Big Willow Canyon and climb to 7,000 feet as the trail crosses back into Big Willow Canyon. Make a level contour through the large pine trees and cross a small stream. Cross another small stream and resume climbing, making a few switchbacks through the dense trees. Break out of the trees into the openness of avalanche debris and small meadows. Climb a couple of glacial moraines and cross through an open stand of quaking aspen trees to reach the stream again. The trail is faint and overgrown here. Stay on the left (north) side of the stream and look for the trail as it switchbacks up the steep slope to the north. Reach a small flat area with an open meadow at 9,500 feet. The trail continues east 0.4 miles to reach the overlook into Bells Canyon. It is not necessary to go all the way to the overlook. The north route to Lone Peak begins just over the moraine to the right (south).

■ Schoolhouse Springs

From the trailhead at 5,300 feet, begin climbing the 4wd road as it switchbacks up the hillside. Follow the main road as it makes four switchbacks to 6,200 feet. At the fifth switchback, the road is blocked by a gate to private property. Go straight (north) and begin climbing steeply to 7,100 feet on a single track and rejoin the 4wd road that has been climbing through private property. Continue on the 4wd road for 2.2 miles to reach the First Hamongog (meadow) at 7,200 feet. A Lone Peak Wilderness sign marks the end of the road and the meadow where the trail forks. Halfway across the meadow, the trail forks. The left fork leads to the Second Hamongog and the south ridge to Lone Peak. The right fork leads to Lake Hardy and the south ridge to South Thunder. Take the left fork and continue climbing to the west on a distinct trail. Initially, climb west and then north toward the second meadow. Reach the second meadow after 3.2 miles at 8,200 feet. The remaining route to Lone Peak is visible to the north.

ROUTES

■ **5.1 North Ridge via Big Willow, Class 4**

From Big Willow Trailhead: 11.0 miles RT; 6,150 feet
From the meadow area at 9,500 feet in Big Willow Canyon, climb up the tree-covered moraine directly to the south. On top of the moraine, the slopes open up to reveal the remaining route. Choose your line of ascent. Leave the trees and venture onto the boulders or consolidated snow in early season. Climb the middle of the slopes slightly right (west) of a small cliff band. The jagged ridge blocking passage into Bells Canyon is directly to your left (east). Climb 1,200 feet up boulders, scree, and broken cliff bands. Toward the top of your ascent, contour (east) and reach the bench directly north of Lone Peak's summit at 10,700 feet.

From the bench on the north ridge at 10,700 feet, begin an ascending traverse east toward the ridge. Gain the ridge at 11,000 feet as Lone Peak's summit comes into view. Contour toward the summit by making an ascending traverse through west-facing boulders. This ascent leads to the north ridge proper as Bells Canyon drops below to the east. Stay along the ridge to the summit from this point. A few hundred feet from the summit, the Class 3 traverse transitions to Class 4 climbing. A large block along the ridge must be negotiated. It is generally bypassed on the left (east) side by down-climbing 10 feet. Once the large block is bypassed, climb out of a small notch to reach the final summit blocks. The actual summit is a flat, appliance-sized

The north ridge of Lone Peak

block. The final moves to the summit are Class 4 and exposed on both sides of the ridge. Stand atop Lone Peak's summit and feel the exhilaration.

■ 5.2 West via Bear Canyon, Class 4

From Orson Smith Trailhead: 12.0 miles RT; 6,450 feet

From the meadow north of Outlaw Cabin at 9,300 feet begin climbing to the east across the meadow. Continue following the drainage east, staying toward the left (north) side of some granite cliffs. The angle gets steeper and the drainage narrows toward the top. Cliffs close in on the east and south. Traverse slightly left (north) through the narrow break in the cliffs. Lone Peak comes into view to the east. Take a mental picture of this area and note a landmark for your return. From the west rim of the cirque, continue contouring east and slightly north to reach the small, flat area north of Lone Peak at 10,700 feet. See Route 5.1 for the final route description.

■ 5.3 West via Draper Ridge or Jacobs Ladder, Class 4

From Draper Ridge Trailhead: 13.6 miles RT; 5,950 feet

From Jacobs Ladder Trailhead: 12.6 miles RT; 5,650 feet

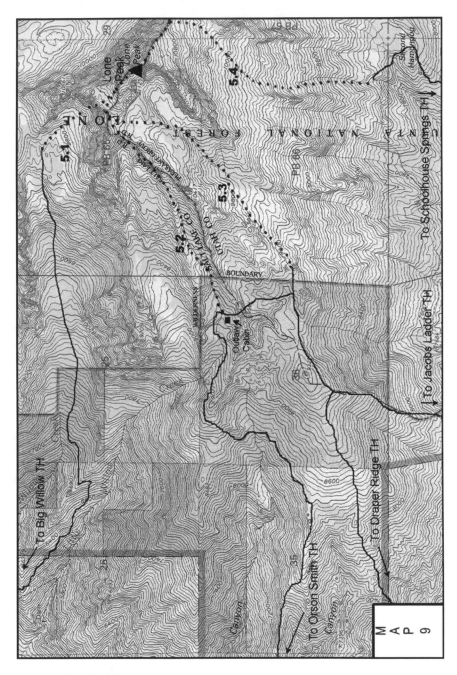

MAP 9. *Lone Peak Routes*

From the Draper Ridge/Jacobs Ladder junction at 9,200 feet, continue east through a meadow and cross a small stream. Do not follow the stream. The route continues east across a ridge and into the southern end of the cirque. Cairns mark the remainder of the route to the cirque west of Lone Peak's summit. The elevation gain is a little over 200 feet from the junction with Draper Ridge and the cirque. The trail enters the south end of the cirque and ends after 4.5 miles. The route generally stays on the right (east) side of the stream. Cross the cirque to reach its northern end. The towering west face of Lone Peak looks over your approach. Aim for the low point on the northern ridge from the north end of the cirque. Climb grassy ledges and granite slabs to reach the north ridge's low point at 10,700 feet. See Route 5.1 for final route description.

▨ 5.4 South via Schoolhouse Springs, Class 3

From Schoolhouse Springs Trailhead: 10.5 miles RT; 5,950 feet

Look north toward Lone Peak from the second meadow at 8,200 feet. There is a cliff band on the left (west), a small cliff band in the middle, and a larger cliff band on the right (east). Cross the second meadow to reach the north end. Traverse left (west) slightly on a visible trail to reach the drainage immediately east of the westernmost cliff band you viewed from the meadow. Climb steeply to 8,900 feet on a faint trail. At 8,900 feet, begin an ascending traverse toward the northeast. This traverse will put you near the top of the middle cliff band you viewed from the meadow. Climb to reach the top of the middle cliff band at 10,000 feet. Turn left (north) toward the ridge and climb broken granite slabs to reach the ridge at 10,700. A cairn marks the spot. Bells Canyon comes into view below. From the ridge turn left (west) and continue ascending. The angle eases and the large blocks give way to open tundra below the south summit of Lone Peak. Ascend the tundra and occasional boulders to gain Lone Peak's south summit at 11,200 feet. Continue Class 3 scrambling along the east side of the ridge a few hundred feet to reach Lone Peak's main summit at 11,243 feet.

6. South Thunder Mountain – 11,154 feet

See maps on pages 38 and 50

South Thunder Mountain is seldom visited. In fact, it is one of the least visited summits in the Wasatch. There is no easy approach to South Thunder. Long approaches are available via Lake Hardy or Bells Canyon or by traversing two miles along the ridge from Pfeifferhorn's summit. Whichever approach you use will be rewarded with a feeling of accomplishment.

TRAILHEADS

■ **Bells Canyon**

This trailhead is at 5,130 feet. If approaching from the south exit I-15 at the 12300 South exit (Exit 291). Turn east and continue 1.8 miles to 1300 East. Continue straight through the intersection as the road winds around to the north. Turn right at the stoplight after 3.0 miles onto Wasatch Boulevard. Drive on Wasatch Boulevard and continue east past Hidden Valley Park after 5.8 miles. Continue north on Wasatch Boulevard and reach the Bells Canyon trailhead after 7.9 miles.

The west face of South Thunder

If approaching from the north, exit I-215 at 6200 South (Exit 6). Turn east toward the mountains and reach the mouth of Big Cottonwood Canyon after 1.6 miles. Continue south on Wasatch Boulevard and turn right after 3.8 miles. Reach the intersection with 9400 South after 4.9 miles. Continue straight (south) and reach the Bells Canyon trailhead after 5.5 miles. Sandy City has constructed an official trailhead at 10275 South Wasatch Boulevard.

▪ Schoolhouse Springs

See page 39 for description

APPROACHES

▪ Bells Canyon

The first two miles of this trail are extremely popular with hikers. It is well maintained and easy to follow. Begin hiking along the fences through the private residential area. Drop down to a creek draining lower Bells Reservoir and continue climbing 450 feet to reach lower Bells Reservoir at 5,550 feet. Contour around the north end of the lake and continue a short distance east on a 4wd road. The 4wd road turns right (south) at a marked junction where the trail turns left (east). Cross to the stream's south side on a sturdy wooden bridge and then pass a Lone Peak Wilderness sign at 5,900 feet after 1.1 miles. Climb steeply to 6,900 feet where the trail makes a switchback, and contour slightly to the east. Resume climbing, turning right (southeast), and climb toward the stream to 7,300 feet. Reach a footbridge crossing to the stream's east side after 2.2 miles. This is a popular destination for many who come to view the spectacular waterfall. Cross the stream and continue climbing on the left (east) side of the stream to reach a meadow area at 7,850 feet after 2.7 miles. Cross the stream back to the west side and resume climbing. The trail becomes faint in places and is overgrown above this point. Look for cairns but don't count on them between this point and the lake. Look for remnants of trail in between cairns and continue climbing the remaining 1,500 feet to upper Bells Reservoir at 9,400 feet.

■ Lake Hardy via Schoolhouse Springs

From the trailhead at 5,300 feet, begin climbing the 4wd road as it switchbacks up the hillside. Follow the main road as it makes four switchbacks to 6,200 feet. At the fifth switchback the road is blocked by a gate to private property. Go straight (north) and begin climbing steeply to 7,100 feet on a single track and rejoin the 4wd road that has been climbing through private property. Continue on the 4wd road to reach the First Hamongog (meadow) at 7,200 feet after 2.2 miles. A Lone Peak Wilderness sign marks the end of the road and the meadow. Halfway across the meadow, the trail forks. The left fork leads to the Second Hamongog and the south ridge to Lone Peak. The right fork leads to Lake Hardy and the south ridge to South Thunder. Take the right fork and climb over a small ridge to reach the reliable creek draining Lake Hardy thousands of feet higher. Continue climbing 0.2 miles as the trail turns left (north) and climbs to reach the Dry Creek cutoff trail at 7,600 feet after 3.0 miles. Climb up the drainage over 1,000 feet on a dry, overgrown trail to the base of cliffs that have been watching over your approach. Look for cairns and transition from trail to open slabs of granite. Make an ascending traverse

Lake Hardy from the east

across the slabs for another 500 feet to reach the creek again at 9,100 feet. The stream marks your transition into a small, narrow canyon with a canopy of old, subalpine fir trees. Follow the stream on its east side to reach a magical meadow at 9,500 feet. Cross the meadow to reach the open slopes at the northwest end of the meadow. Climb 500 feet along the left (west) side of the drainage. Immediately below the lake reach some rounded granite slabs toward the middle of the drainage. Ascend the rounded slabs and reach Lake Hardy at 10,000 feet. This is a pristine place which has seen some abuse from campers in the past. Camp at least 200 feet away from the lake should you choose to stay and fully appreciate the beauty of this place.

ROUTES

■ **6.1 West Ridge via Bells Canyon, Class 3**

From Bells Canyon Trailhead: 12.0 miles RT; 6,025 feet

From upper Bells Canyon Reservoir, climb around the west end of the lake. Stay high to avoid cliffs on the lake's west side. Your objective is to reach the small notch above the lake's south end. A cairn marks this spot. From this notch above the south end of Upper Bells Reservoir, contour under the cliffs to the east. Stay close to the cliffs and watch for another cairn after 0.2 miles. This cairn is important because it marks the beginning of the easiest break in the cliff band. Turn left (east) and begin climbing open granite slabs toward South Thunder. South Thunder's west face soon comes into view. If you have chosen the right line of ascent, you will soon arrive directly under the west face of South Thunder. Leave the relative comfort of the chute and cross right (south) under the west face to reach the west ridge. Gain the ridge a few hundred feet below South Thunder's summit. The final boulders are surprisingly pleasant as they provide 10- to 15-foot ramps that facilitate your ascent. Reach the summit and a mailbox register at 11,154 feet.

■ **6.2 South Ridge via Lake Hardy, Class 2**

From Schoolhouse Springs Trailhead: 11.5 miles RT; 5,850 feet

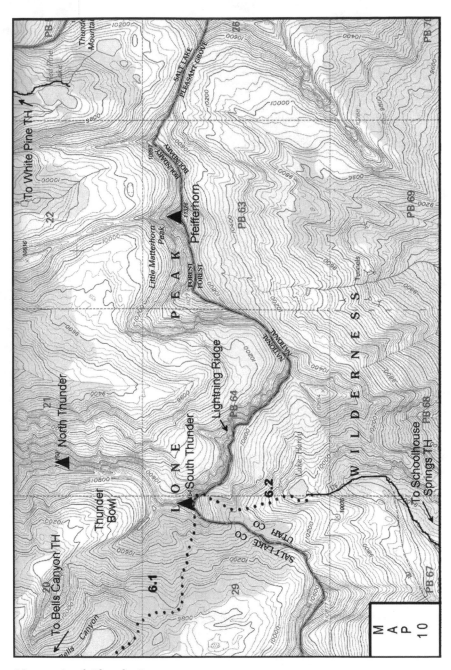

MAP 10. *South Thunder Routes*

From Lake Hardy contour around the west side of the lake to reach a boulder field on the lake's north end. Climb the boulder field, aiming for the middle of the boulder field. Climb an open granite slab to reach the ridge with Bells Canyon. Turn right (east) and climb 500 feet on open tundra to reach the south shoulder of South Thunder at 11,000 feet. South Thunder dominates your view to the left (north) a short distance away. Traverse north along the ridge and climb the final boulders 150 feet to reach South Thunder's summit. The south ridge can be gained a number of ways, Lake Hardy being only one option. The south shoulder can also be reached as part of the Beatout Traverse from Pfeifferhorn. It can also be reached by climbing all the way up Bells Canyon to the divide at 10,500 feet and then traveling east along the ridge.

7. North Thunder Mountain – 11,150 feet

See maps on pages 38 and 52

Only a handful of people venture to North Thunder's summit each year. In fact, during the last two years only a dozen people have signed the register. The summit is guarded well by long, difficult approaches. Most people climb North Thunder by traversing from South Thunder and then return to exit via Bells Canyon. Others choose to traverse back across the Beatout Traverse to Pfeifferhorn and return to White Pine trailhead. Choose your approach and route wisely and become one of the elite to sit atop North Thunder.

TRAILHEAD

■ Bells Canyon

See page 46 for description

APPROACH

■ Bells Canyon

The first two miles of this trail are extremely popular with hikers. It is well maintained and easy to follow. Begin hiking along the fences through the private residential area. Drop down to a creek draining

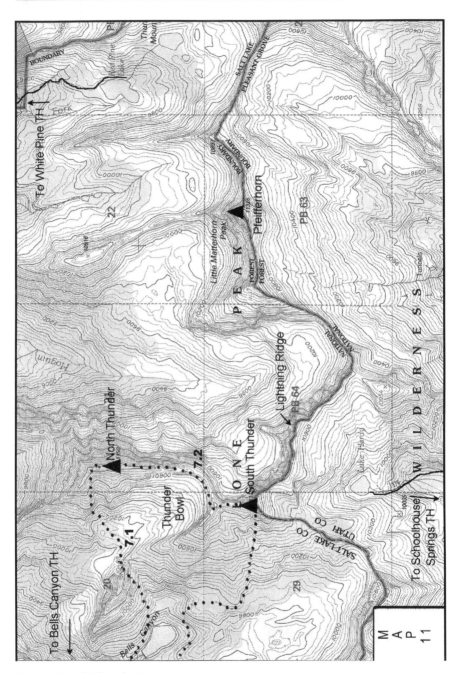

Map 11. *North Thunder Routes*

lower Bells Reservoir and continue climbing 450 feet to reach lower Bells Reservoir at 5,550 feet. Contour around to the left (north) end of the lake and continue a short distance east on the 4wd road. The 4wd road turns right (south) at a marked junction where the trail turns left (east). Cross to the stream's south side on a sturdy wooden bridge and then pass a Lone Peak Wilderness sign at 5,900 feet after 1.1 miles. Climb steeply to 6,900 feet where the trail makes a switch-back, and contour slightly to the east. Resume climbing, turning right (southeast), and climb toward the stream at 7,300 feet. Reach a foot-bridge crossing to the stream's left (east) side after 2.2 miles. This is a popular destination for many who come to view the spectacular waterfall. Cross the stream and continue climbing on the east side of the stream to reach a meadow area at 7,850 feet after 2.7 miles. Cross the stream back to the west side and resume climbing. The trail becomes faint in places and is overgrown above this point. Look for cairns but don't count on them between this point and the lake. Look for remnants of trail in between cairns and continue climbing the remaining 1,500 feet to upper Bells Reservoir at 9,400 feet.

ROUTES

■ **7.1 West Slopes, Class 3**

From Bells Canyon Trailhead: 9.8 miles RT; 6,020 feet

The west slopes of North Thunder can be reached from upper Bells Reservoir. From the north end of the lake, engage the broken cliff bands to the left (east). By carefully choosing your route, you can keep the difficulty to Class 3. Ascend the broken cliff bands, aiming for a notch on the ridge at 10,200 feet. Thunder Bowl and North Thunder come into view to the east. Drop 200 feet through large boulders and a broken cliff band to reach the south shores of a small lake at 10,000 feet. Look east and aim for the low point on the ridge immediately left (north) of North Thunder's summit. Climb a short, Class 3 chute to reach the ridge. From the ridge turn right (south) and scramble a short distance on the Class 3 ridge to reach North Thunder's summit.

The Thunder Traverse with Twin Peaks Wilderness as background

▪ 7.2 The Thunder Traverse, Class 3

From Pfeifferhorn & Bells Canyon descent: 12.0 miles one-way; 4,800 feet gain & 7,200 feet loss

From Bells Canyon Trailhead: 12.0 miles RT; 6,500 feet

The most popular way of completing this traverse is by approaching via the Beatout Traverse (see page 58) from Pfeifferhorn and descending Bells Canyon. Ascending Bells Canyon to South Thunder, completing the traverse, and descending Bells Canyon is the second most popular way. From South Thunder's summit, descend the north slopes to 10,800 feet. Ascend 100 feet to reach Thunder Bowl's south ridge. Descend Class 3 terrain 100 feet to bypass some cliffs on the south ridge of Thunder Bowl. Traverse at 10,800 feet, aiming for some trees along the ridge. Climb toward the trees, through a cliff band, and gain the ridge again at 11,000 feet after 0.7 miles. Traverse left (north) another 0.2 miles to reach North Thunder's summit at 11,150 feet.

8. The Pfeifferhorn – 11,326 feet

See maps on pages 38 and 57

The Pfeifferhorn, known as Little Matterhorn on some topographical maps, resembles the real Matterhorn on a smaller scale. The triangular summit is impressive when viewed from most any vantage point. A relatively easy route from Red Pine Lake compared to other Lone Peak Wilderness peaks motivates many to climb it. Red Pine Lake via White Pine trailhead provides the main and most popular access. The Pfeifferhorn provides the launching point for the Beatout Traverse to South Thunder Mountain.

TRAILHEAD

▪ White Pine

This trailhead at 7,600 feet is located 0.7 miles west of Snowbird Ski Resort. From the north, exit I-215 at 6200 South (Exit 6). Turn east toward the mountains and continue 1.6 miles to the mouth of Big Cottonwood Canyon. Go straight through the intersection, following signs for Alta and Snowbird Ski Resorts. Reach the electric notification sign after 5.4 miles at the mouth of Little Cottonwood Canyon.

If approaching from the south, exit I-15 at 9000 South (Exit 295). Turn east and continue 6.0 miles to Wasatch Boulevard. Go straight and reach the electric notification sign at the mouth of Little Cottonwood Canyon after 7.2 miles. Measuring from this point, continue east past the popular rock climbing areas in lower Little Cottonwood

The Pfeifferhorn viewed from the east

Canyon and past the power plant at 1.8 miles. The Tanners Flat Campground is reached after 4.2 miles. Continue east and reach White Pine trailhead after 5.2 miles. White Pine trailhead is easy to miss since the turn is immediately after a blind turn in the road.

APPROACH

■ Red Pine Lake via White Pine Trailhead

This approach is very popular and Red Pine Lake is a desired destination for many. From the south end of the White Pine trailhead, follow a paved footpath down the hill to a well-constructed footbridge across the stream. Cross the stream and turn right (west). The trail is an old jeep road that climbs gradually up the hill in a southwesterly direction. It climbs into the White Pine Canyon drainage and turns left (south) to reach the junction with the Red Pine Canyon trail after 1.0 miles. The White Pine trail makes a sharp switchback left (east) at the junction. The Red Pine trail crosses the stream 50 feet upstream (south) on a small footbridge. Once across the stream, continue downstream for 50 yards and then gradually ascend west around the end of the ridge to a Lone Peak Wilderness sign. Continue southwest to reach an overlook offering views down Little Cottonwood Canyon. The overlook is at 8,200 feet and 1.5 miles from the trailhead. From the overlook climb 900 feet in the next mile to reach the junction with the Maybird Gulch trail that begins climbing to the west. From the Maybird Gulch trail junction, continue climbing the steep Red Pine trail 540 feet for the next 0.9 miles. The trail is well-worn and generally stays in the trees on the eastern side of the drainage. A small spur ridge separates the trail from the creek. Reach Red Pine Lake at 9,640 feet after 3.4 miles.

ROUTE

■ 8.1 East Ridge, Class 3

From White Pine Trailhead: 9.0 miles RT; 3,725 feet

At Red Pine Lake continue around the east side to the inlet on the south end near a large boulder. Follow the stream as it climbs through

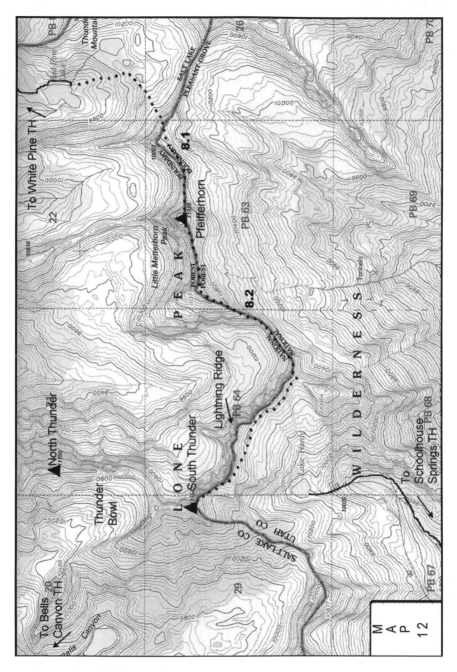

MAP 12. *The Pfeifferhorn and Beatout Traverse Routes*

the trees toward a spur ridge. Climb to the spur ridge that runs south-west toward the main ridge. Staying on the spur ridge, you can glimpse upper Red Pine Lake as you emerge from the trees. Continue along the spur ridge to gain the main ridge at 10,700 feet. The head-wall beneath the ridge is steep. Spring climbs require an ice axe and crampons, and a cornice may be present. From the ridge at the top of the headwall, turn right (west). Pfeifferhorn welcomes your presence as it dominates the western skyline. Traverse along the south side of the ridge past two minor summits. Pass the second minor summit and let the climbing begin. Scramble onto the ridge and pick through the large boulders and blocks. Halfway across the ridge, the largest blocks hinder easy progress. These blocks can be bypassed on the right (north) by down-climbing 10 feet and traversing underneath them, then gaining the ridge again. Continue along the ridge to the base of the final summit pyramid. Climb the east-facing slopes, stay-ing 10 to 20 feet from the easternmost ridge. Continue Class 2 climb-ing to reach the summit at 11,326 feet.

■ 8.2 The Beatout Traverse, Class 3

From White Pine Trailhead & Bells Canyon Descent: 12.5 miles total; 4,330 feet gain, 6,800 feet loss

A car shuttle may be needed for this traverse. After reaching Pfeiffer-horn's summit, most people enjoy the views, then turn around and return to White Pine trailhead. Others choose to begin the Beatout Traverse. If you are one of them, drop down Pfeifferhorn's west ridge 320 feet to reach the saddle between Unnamed 11,137 and the Pfeiffer-horn. Either climb up and over Unnamed 11,137 or contour under its southeast slope at 11,000 feet. Continue along the ridge to reach its low point at 10,550 feet. It is possible to stay on the ridge, but the easi-est route drops left (south) off the ridge about 50 feet. Contour for a few hundred feet slightly below the ridge to reach the final climb to the Chipman Peak saddle. Class 3 climbing for 300 feet up loose boul-ders offers a view of the Chipman Peak saddle. Climb another 50 feet along the ridge and contour to Chipman's saddle at 10,800 feet. Wel-come to Lightning Ridge, which runs between Chipman Peak's sad-dle and South Thunder. It no doubt gets its name from the remnants

The Beatout Traverse

The Pfeifferhorn viewed from the Beatout Traverse to the west

of charred trees from numerous lightning strikes. From Chipman Peak's saddle, a short out and back along the ridge to the south leads to Chipman Peak's summit at 10,954 feet. Choosing not to make the short side-trip to Chipman leaves you with another choice. Either stay along the ridge or drop about 50 to 100 feet below the ridge to make the traverse to the south shoulder of South Thunder. The ridge involves scrambling over huge boulders crowning the head of Hogum Fork to the north. Below the ridge involves navigating large, open slabs of granite. Pick your preference and gain the south shoulder of South Thunder, then climb the south ridge to reach the summit. Leave the summit and descend the west slopes to a point 0.2 miles south of Upper Bells Reservoir. Descend Bells Canyon 5.0 miles and 4,100 feet. Lake Hardy may also be used as a descent for the Beatout Traverse. A descent via Lake Hardy or Bells Canyon will require a car shuttle to return to White Pine trailhead.

9. White Baldy – 11,321 feet

See maps on pages 38 and 62

White Baldy forms the eastern edge of the Lone Peak Wilderness. Both main approaches are popular with hikers. Red Pine and White Pine Lakes attract many hikers each year. Few venture beyond White Pine Lake. Both the east and west ridges require scrambling and guard White Baldy's summit well.

TRAILHEAD

▪ **White Pine**

See page 55 for description

APPROACHES

▪ **White Pine Lake via White Pine Trailhead**

From the south end of the White Pine trailhead, follow a paved footpath down the hill to a well-constructed footbridge across the stream. Cross the stream and turn right (west). The trail is an old jeep road that climbs gradually up the hill in a southwesterly direction. It climbs into the White Pine Canyon drainage and turns left (south) to

White Baldy view from upper White Pine Canyon

reach the junction with the Red Pine Canyon trail after 1.0 miles. Follow the road, which makes a sharp switchback left to an overlook at 1.5 miles. Continue past two more switchbacks and arrive at a nice meadow at 8,500 feet after 2.0 miles. Above the meadow the trail makes a series of short switchbacks along the left (east) side of the drainage. It eventually climbs over a spur ridge, and White Pine Lake comes into view. The road continues a short distance to White Pine Lake at 10,000 feet after 5.0 miles.

■ **Red Pine Lake via White Pine Trailhead**

See page 56 for description

ROUTES

■ **9.1 East Ridge via White Pine Lake, Class 3**

From White Pine Trailhead: 11.0 miles RT; 3,720 feet

Leave the 4wd road at 10,200 feet before it makes the last turn to drop down to White Pine Lake. Continue straight (south) onto the boulder field and begin contouring toward the ridge. Contour along the boulder field and cross a small moraine. Begin ascending loose boulders or snow in early season and make a gradual ascent across the boulder

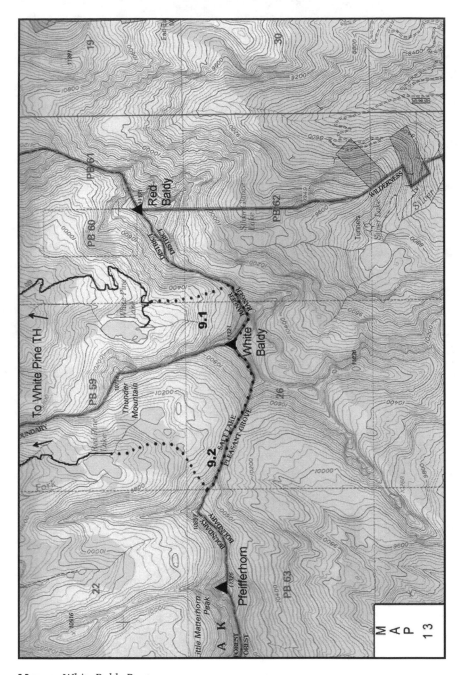

Map 13. *White Baldy Routes*

White Pine Lake with Mount Superior and Monte Cristo as background

field, continuing south. Aim for a notch right (west) of the low point on the ridge. A small, tooth-like formation on the ridge makes a good target. It is not necessary to go all the way to the ridge. Within a hundred feet of the ridge, continue an ascending traverse of the boulders and scree on the north face of White Baldy. A cliff along the ridge is soon visible. Climb toward the ridge and gain it directly east of the ridge's cliffs. A ramp continues along the north side of the cliffs. Once past this obstacle, gain the ridge and continue along the ridge where possible. White Baldy's summit soon comes into view. Cross to the left (south) side of the ridge when easy passage is not possible on the ridge proper. The rock is solid on the left (south) side of the ridge. The initial ridge is Class 2 with loose boulders and scree. The final few hundred feet to the summit are on solid Class 3 rock.

■ 9.2 West Ridge via Red Pine Lake, Class 3

From White Pine Trailhead: 10.5 miles RT; 4,120 feet

At Red Pine Lake continue around the left (east) side to the inlet on the south end near a large boulder. Follow the stream as it climbs through the trees toward a spur ridge. Climb to the spur ridge that runs southwest toward the main ridge. Stay on the spur ridge and view upper Red Pine Lake as you emerge from the trees. Continue along the spur ridge to gain the main ridge at 10,700 feet. The headwall beneath the ridge is steep. Spring climbs require an ice axe and crampons, and a cornice may be present. From the ridge at the top of the headwall, turn left (east). Begin a Class 2 descent to reach the low point along the west ridge at 10,500 feet after 0.5 miles. Obstacles along the ridge are generally bypassed on the right (south) side of the ridge. Climb 700 feet to reach the false west summit of White Baldy. The ridge from Dry Creek Divide joins here. Turn left (northeast) and continue the Class 3 traverse to reach White Baldy's summit after a short scramble.

10. Box Elder Peak – 11,101 feet

See maps on pages 38 and 67

Box Elder is the red-headed stepchild of the Lone Peak Wilderness. Someone always asks, "What is that peak over there?" Most people recognize the other Wasatch peaks and can easily point out Mount Timpanogos to the south. Box Elder is always somewhere in between. It lies south of the main cluster of Lone Peak Group peaks and north of Mount Timpanogos. It is easier than any other Lone Peak Group peak by both distance and difficulty. Approaches are shorter and a Class 2 stroll takes you to the summit. Notwithstanding, Box Elder is a majestic peak with a huge northwest-facing bowl which is home to dozens of mountain goats. Take a day and enjoy what Box Elder has to offer.

TRAILHEADS

■ **Dry Creek**

This trailhead is at 5,650 feet and provides access to Box Elder's north ridge. From I-15 south of Salt Lake City and north of Provo, take Exit 284 for the town of Alpine. Turn east on Highway 92 and continue to a stoplight at 5300 West after 5.5 miles. Turn left (north) and drive 8.7 miles to reach Grove Drive in the town of Alpine. Grove Drive

Box Elder Peak viewed from Dry Creek Divide

winds north and east for another 2.3 miles to reach the Dry Creek trailhead. The trail leaves from the east end of the parking area and is well marked.

▪ Deer Creek

This trailhead is at 6,960 feet and provides access to Box Elder's north ridge. From I-15 south of Salt Lake City and north of Provo, take Exit 284 for the town of Alpine. Turn east onto Highway 92 and continue east to reach a fee booth in American Fork Canyon after 3.0 miles. The vehicle fee of $3 in 2005 is subject to change. Continue east through American Fork Canyon to reach the north fork junction and Highway 144 after 12.2 miles. Turn left (north) and reach Tibble Fork Reservoir after 14.5 miles. Turn left and continue on the paved road to Granite Flat Campground at 15.5 miles. The trailhead and parking is just inside the campground on the right (north) side of the road.

APPROACHES

■ Dry Creek

Dry Creek is a popular trail for horseback riders and is wide, rocky, and loose in places. From the east end of the parking lot, climb 100 feet to reach the Lone Peak Wilderness sign. Reach a reliable creek at 6,750 feet after 1.4 miles. Cross another creek at 7,000 feet. Reach the North Mountain Fork trail junction after 2.0 miles. This junction is at 7,500 feet. Continue climbing and cross the creek at 8,100 feet after 3.0 miles. Quaking aspen and pine trees accompany you on your ascent. Cross the creek again at 8,700 feet. Pfeifferhorn and White Baldy are prominent on the skyline to the north. Leave the creek and climb another 1,000 feet to reach Dry Creek Divide at 9,640 feet. The trail ascending Deer Creek from the east joins at the divide.

■ Deer Creek

This trailhead is at 6,960 feet, with a Lone Peak Wilderness sign just inside the Granite Flat campground on the right. The lower trailhead converges with a spur trail coming in from the south after 0.3 miles. Climb gradually, crossing a stream after 0.8 miles. Soon after crossing the stream, make a switchback right (north) and begin climbing. Box Elder Peak is visible to the southwest during the entire approach. Continue climbing switchbacks across the south-facing slopes and eventually climb to a grassy saddle after 2.8 miles. This grassy saddle at 9,640 feet is the Dry Creek Divide. Deer Creek trail is joined by the Dry Creek trail making its ascent from the town of Alpine. The Pfeifferhorn is visible on the ridgeline to the northwest.

ROUTE

■ 10.1 North Ridge, Class 2

From Dry Creek Trailhead: 14.0 miles RT; 5,650 feet

From Deer Creek Trailhead: 9.6 miles RT; 4,300 feet

Leave the Dry Creek Divide and turn left (south). Follow the ridge for 0.5 miles over two minor summits. Lose 180 feet of elevation to reach

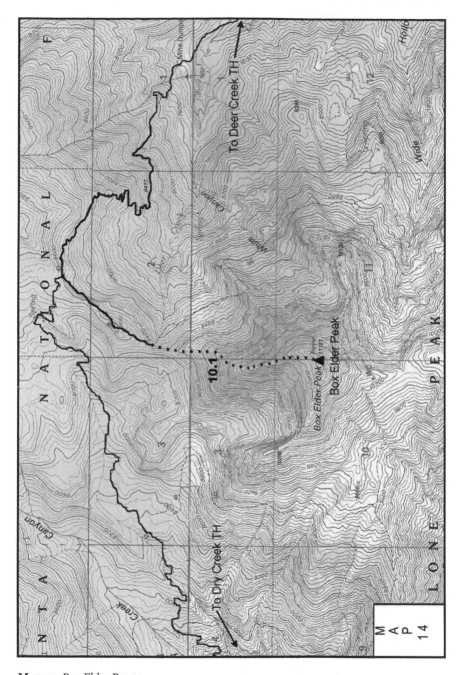

MAP 14. *Box Elder Route*

the saddle just below the north slopes of Box Elder Peak. From this saddle the climbing begins. The trail is faint and often reduced to game trails. Follow the path of least resistance and begin climbing steeply. Wind through trees, staying close to the ridge on the ascent. Continue climbing steeply above the tree line and gain the rocky ridge. The angle eases as Box Elder's summit comes into view again. Continue along the gentle ridge climbing south to reach Box Elder's summit at 11,101 feet.

3

Resort Group

Introduction

The Resort Group includes four peaks around the Alta and Snowbird Ski Resorts, as well as the Bullion Traverse from Sugarloaf to White Baldy. The main attraction is the high point of Salt Lake County, American Fork Twin Peaks. American Fork Twin Peaks, along with its eastern neighbors, Mount Baldy and Sugarloaf, are visited frequently and access is easily gained via wide 4wd service roads used by the resorts. Red Baldy, on the other hand, is seldom visited and often confused with other "red-topped" high points along the alpine ridge.

11. American Fork Twin Peaks – 11,489 feet & 11,433 feet

See maps on pages 72 and 74

Left to right: *Sugarloaf, American Fork Twin Peaks, and Mount Baldy*

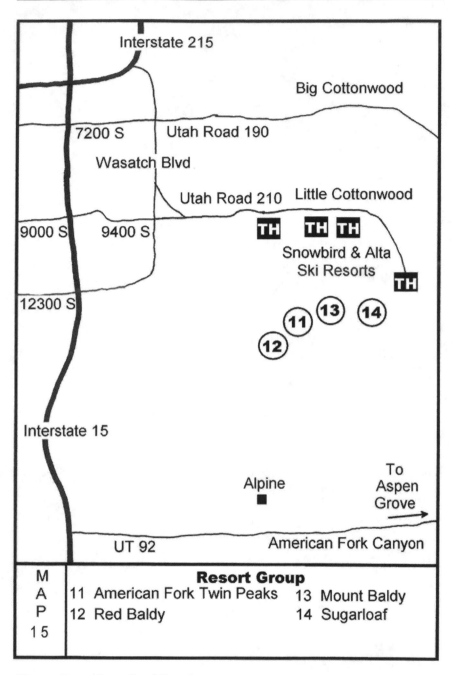

MAP 15. *Resort Group Road Overview*

American Fork Twin Peaks with Hidden Peak in the foreground

As the highest point of Salt Lake County, American Fork Twin Peaks reigns supreme, and many seek its summit. Some compromise the mountain and ride the Snowbird Tram to the top of Hidden Peak (10,995 feet). Somehow justice is served as a knife-edge ridge hinders easy passage between Hidden Peak and American Fork Twin Peaks. The north face is impressive when viewed from upper Gad Valley to the north. However you decide to approach American Fork Twin Peaks, approach with respect. She has earned it.

TRAILHEAD

■ Snowbird Resort Trailhead

This trailhead is at 8,100 feet and is located at the Snowbird Resort Center. If approaching from the north, exit I-215 at 6200 South (Exit 6). Turn east toward the mountains and continue 1.6 miles to the mouth of Big Cottonwood Canyon. Go straight through the intersection following signs for Alta and Snowbird Ski Resorts. Reach the electric notification sign at the mouth of Little Cottonwood Canyon after 5.4 miles.

If approaching from the south, exit I-15 at 9000 South (Exit 295). Turn east and continue 6.0 miles to Wasatch Boulevard. Go straight and reach the electric notification sign at the mouth of Little Cottonwood Canyon after 7.2 miles. Measuring from this point, continue

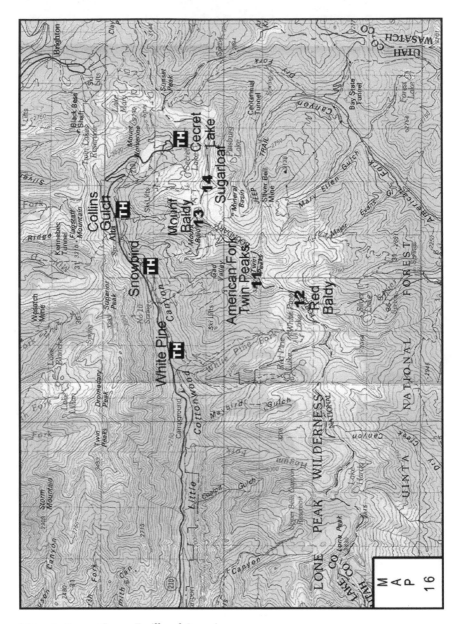

Map 16. *Resort Group Trailhead Overview*

east past the popular rock-climbing areas in lower Little Cottonwood Canyon and pass the power plant at 1.8 miles. The Tanners Flat Campground is reached after 4.2 miles. Continue east past White Pine trailhead at 5.2 miles, pass entry 1 to Snowbird Ski resort and reach Snowbird Entry 2 after 6.3 miles. Turn right and proceed to the parking area immediately west of the Snowbird Resort Center.

APPROACH

■ **Gad Valley**

A Snowbird area map may be helpful, as trails and roads are subject to change. From the Snowbird Tram loading area, cross a small footbridge and reach a trail running along the south side of the stream. Just left (east) of the footbridge, join the trail coming from the Snowbird Center. Turn right on this trail as it runs along Dick Bass Highway trail. The trail climbs under Wilbre Ski Lift and eventually forks. Take the right fork and continue uphill. This road climbs past Mid-Gad Restaurant (closed in summer) near the base of Little Cloud Ski Lift. The trail forks again, and the left fork continues climbing the 4wd service road 1,400 feet toward Hidden Peak and the northeast ridge (Route 11.2). For Route 11.1 take the right fork as it climbs up the Election ski run and ascends a steep, grassy slope. Climb the slopes to the top of Gad 2 ski lift. American Fork Twin's northern face will impress you.

ROUTES

■ **11.1 North Ridge, Class 3**

From Snowbird Resort Trailhead: 8.0 miles RT; 3,550 feet

From the top of Gad 2 ski lift, the entire northern ridge is visible to the right (west). Pick your line of ascent. Generally, the easiest way to gain the ridge is to follow a service road to the right (west) a short distance. Look toward the southwest and find a small break in the trees after 50 yards. Follow a small, grass-covered drainage to reach the boulders at the base of the ridge. Ascend the boulders 400 feet to gain the northern ridge of 10,500 feet. The views into White Pine Canyon and the other peaks to the west open up. Turn left (south)

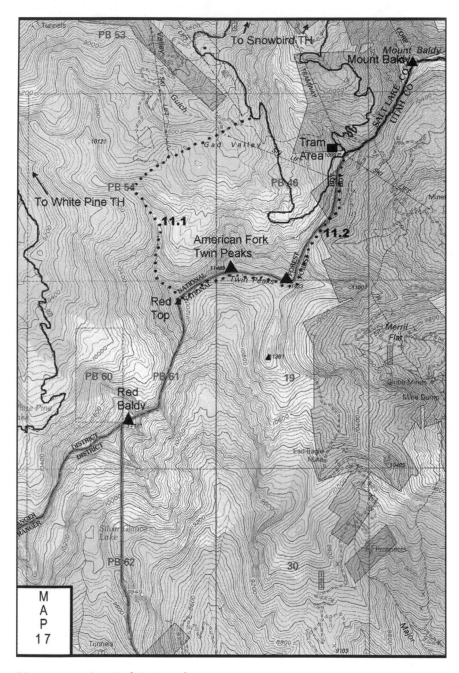

Map 17. *American Fork Twin Peaks Routes*

and follow the ridge for Class 2 climbing to the top of a minor summit west of American Fork Twin Peaks' west summit at 11,171 feet. This point is known as Red Top Mountain, but is unnamed on topographic maps. Turn left (east) and lose 150 feet to reach the small saddle west of American Fork Twin's western summit. Climb the remaining 260 feet to reach the summit and high point of Salt Lake County.

▨ 11.2 Northeast Ridge, Class 4

From Snowbird Resort Trailhead: 8.0 miles RT; 3,400 feet

The northeast ridge is knife-edge and the rocks are sharp. This ridge intimidates a lot of people and has a reputation for being extremely difficult. No doubt much of this reputation has been erroneously perpetuated by less-experienced hikers who have tried the ridge because of its ease of access. Many tourists ride the tram and go for a short walk that brings them to this ridge. For the uninitiated and inexperienced, climbing the ridge may be challenging. For others, it offers a thrill. Either way, it will be memorable.

From the saddle immediately west of Hidden Peak at 10,850 feet, leave the service road and gain the ridge. A climber's trail leaves from the service road and climbs 30 feet to the ridge proper. At first, the trail seems harmless as it winds through trees and around larger rocks. After 100 yards the trail drops 10 feet to engage the ridge. The scrambling begins. Generally, it is easiest to stay on the ridge proper. Strong cross winds can challenge your equilibrium. Bolts have been placed in strategic locations on the ridge for those choosing to use a belay. Dance along the top of the knife-edge, gaining little elevation initially on lighter colored rock. Generally, the ridge is Class 3–4. Some Class 5 moves may be necessary to negotiate some boulders or to compensate for previous poor route-finding decisions. Once across the lighter colored rock, transition to darker colored rock as the ridge begins to gain elevation. The darker rock looks intimidating, but the climbing difficulty eases to consistent Class 3. Ascend the darker colored rock to reach light-colored scree on the east slopes. Contour left (south) immediately above a cliff band and follow the series of trails worn into the slope. Generally, the best trail is on the southeast side instead of the east side proper.

12. Red Baldy – 11,171 feet

See maps on pages 72 and 79

Quiet and secure, Red Baldy rests between White Baldy and American Fork Twin Peaks. The other peaks attract the climbers. Red Baldy may be seldom visited because it is the benefactor of some confusion. Many confuse Red Top Mountain (11,171 feet) immediately west of American Fork Twin Peaks' west summit for Red Baldy. In fact, U.S. Forest Service maps even have it mislabeled on one of their trail maps. The real Red Baldy rests immediately east of White Baldy along the ridge.

TRAILHEAD

▪ White Pine

This trailhead is at 7,600 feet, 0.75 miles west of Snowbird Resort. If approaching from the north, exit I-215 at 6200 South (Exit 6). Turn east toward the mountains and continue 1.6 miles to the mouth of Big Cottonwood Canyon. Go straight through the intersection following signs for Alta and Snowbird Ski Resorts. Reach the electric notification sign at the mouth of Little Cottonwood Canyon after 5.4 miles.

If approaching from the south exit I-15 at 9000 South (Exit 295). Turn east and continue 6.0 miles to Wasatch Boulevard. Go straight and reach the electric notification sign at the mouth of Little Cottonwood Canyon after 7.2 miles. Measuring from this point, continue east past the popular rock-climbing areas in lower Little Cottonwood Canyon and pass the power plant at 1.8 miles. The Tanners Flat Campground is reached after 4.2 miles. Continue east and reach White Pine trailhead after 5.2 miles. White Pine trailhead is easy to miss since the turn is immediately after a blind turn in the road.

APPROACH

▪ White Pine Lake

From the south end of White Pine trailhead, follow a paved footpath down the hill to a well-constructed footbridge across the stream. Cross the stream and turn right (west). The trail is an old jeep road that climbs gradually up the hill in a southwesterly direction. It

Red Baldy viewed from the northeast ridge

climbs into the White Pine Canyon drainage and turns south to reach the junction with the Red Pine Canyon trail after 1.0 miles. Follow the road, which makes a sharp switchback left (east). Reach an overlook at 8,500 feet after two switchbacks. The road turns south and climbs slightly to reach a nice meadow area at 8,600 feet after 2.0 miles. Above the meadow make a series of short switchbacks and climb along the east side of the drainage. Climb through a stand of trees to reach another small meadow, then cross a creek and climb over a small spur ridge. Contour east toward the creek. The northeast route (Route 12.2) to Red Baldy begins here at 9,800 feet beneath the north cliffs of Red Baldy. Continue along the road over another spur ridge to reach the open boulder field below White Pine Lake.

Make several more smaller switchbacks before making one long switchback under the west slopes of Red Baldy. The northwest route (Route 12.1) begins here at 10,000 feet at the beginning of the last long switchback. To reach White Pine Lake, continue climbing on the road in a southwesterly direction to a stand of trees at 10,200 feet. White Pine Lake comes into view to the west. Route 12.3 leaves the road from this small stand of trees. The road continues and drops the final 200 feet to reach the lake after 5.0 miles.

ROUTES

▪ 12.1 Northwest Slopes, Class 2

From White Pine Lake Trailhead: 8.0 miles RT; 3,570 feet

Leave the 4wd road at 10,000 feet. The road makes one last switchback to White Pine Lake from this point. Engage the west slope of Red Baldy on mixed terrain of tundra and rocks. Ascend the tundra toward trees marking the beginning of the northwest ridge. Don't be tempted to turn for the summit of Red Baldy too soon. Climb in a northeasterly direction to reach the top of the ridge at 10,750 feet. Leave the comfort of the tundra and climb along the rocks along the ridge south toward Red Baldy's summit. This terrain is Class 2 along the ridge. Climb the remaining 400 feet to reach Red Baldy's east (higher) summit at 11,171 feet. A short scramble on Class 3 rock leads to Red Baldy's west summit which is a few feet shorter.

▪ 12.2 Northeast Ridge, Class 4

From White Pine Lake Trailhead: 8.0 miles RT; 3,570 feet

Leave the 4wd road at 9,800 feet. This point is next to the stream directly below the north cliffs of Red Baldy. Cross the stream and climb granite slabs to the east. From the top of the slabs, the saddle between Red Top Mountain and Red Baldy comes into view. Cross the boulder field to the east and reach the saddle at 10,550 feet. The entire northeast ridge comes into view, and it looks intimidating. The rock quality is generally better on the ridge. At times, descend about 10 feet on the ridge's left (southeast) side to climb around large blocks

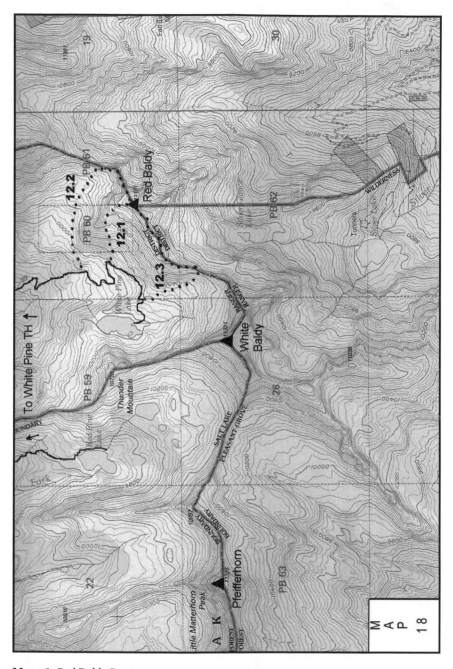

MAP 18. *Red Baldy Routes*

on the ridge. Climb to a notch at 10,800 feet, then climb to the left around the vertical rock in the notch and gain the ridge again. Climb Class 4 terrain and admire the exposure to your right (north). Reach Red Baldy's east (higher) summit at 11,171 feet. A short scramble on Class 3 rock leads to Red Baldy's west summit which is a few feet shorter.

■ 12.3 West Ridge, Class 3

From White Pine Lake Trailhead: 9.2 miles RT; 3,570 feet

Leave the 4wd road from a stand of trees before the road drops 200 feet to reach White Pine Lake. Initially, climb through the trees and cross a small stretch of boulders. Aim for a point along the ridge left (east) of the actual low point. Climb directly under the west cliffs of Red Baldy on mixed rock and tundra to avoid endless boulder hopping. Climb left (east) of a stand of small trees to reach the saddle between Red Baldy and White Baldy at 10,700 feet. Turn left (east) and climb along the south side of the ridge to reach an unnamed 11,050-foot white granite point along the ridge. Continue east as the rock transitions from white granite to red quartzite. Reach Red Baldy's west (lower) summit. Continue a short, Class 3 scramble to reach Red Baldy's east summit at 11,171 feet.

13. Mount Baldy – 11,068 feet

See maps on pages 72 and 83

Those who say they have climbed an 11,000-foot peak usually mean they have climbed Mount Baldy. Of the "Baldys," this one is a walk in the park for most. It is approached via wide 4wd service roads and has walk-up trails from both the east and west to the summit. It is named. It is above 11,000 feet. It must be climbed.

TRAILHEADS

■ Snowbird Resort

See page 71 for description

Mount Baldy from the east

■ Collins Gulch

This trailhead is at 8,400 feet and provides access to Sugarloaf's west ridge and Mount Baldy's east ridge. If approaching from the north, exit I-215 at 6200 South (Exit 6). Turn east toward the mountains and continue 1.6 miles to the mouth of Big Cottonwood Canyon. Go straight through the intersection following signs for Alta and Snowbird Ski Resorts. Reach the electric notification sign at the mouth of Little Cottonwood Canyon after 5.4 miles.

If approaching from the south, exit I-15 at 9000 South (Exit 295). Turn east and continue 6.0 miles to Wasatch Boulevard. Go straight and reach the electric notification sign at the mouth of Little Cottonwood Canyon after 7.2 miles. Measuring from this point, continue east past the popular rock-climbing area in lower Little Cottonwood Canyon and pass the power plant at 1.8 miles. The Tanners Flat Campground is reached after 4.2 miles. Continue east past White Pine trailhead at 5.2 miles. Pass all four entries to Snowbird and continue east to the town of Alta. Turn right at 8.0 miles into the main parking entrance for Alta Ski Resort. Parking is available near the Goldminers Daughter Restaurant. The trail begins at the southeast corner of the parking lot at the base of the Collins and Wildcat ski lifts.

■ **Cecret (Secret) Lake**

This is the highest trailhead in this book at 9,400 feet. If approaching from the north, exit I-215 at 6200 South (Exit 6). Turn east toward the mountains and continue 1.6 miles to the mouth of Big Cottonwood Canyon. Go straight through the intersection following signs for Alta and Snowbird Ski Resorts. Reach the electric notification sign at the mouth of Little Cottonwood Canyon after 5.4 miles.

If approaching from the south, exit I-15 at 9000 South (Exit 295). Turn east and continue 6.0 miles to Wasatch Boulevard. Go straight and reach the electric notification sign at the mouth of Little Cottonwood Canyon after 7.2 miles. Measuring from this point, continue east past the popular rock-climbing areas in lower Little Cottonwood Canyon and pass the power plant at 1.8 miles. The Tanners Flat Campground is reached after 4.2 miles. Continue east past White Pine trailhead at 5.2 miles. Pass all four entries to Snowbird and continue east through the town of Alta at 8.0 miles. A booth monitoring traffic into Albion Basin is reached after 8.3 miles and the pavement ends at 8.5 miles. The Albion Basin road is closely guarded and regulated. The speed limit is 15 miles per hour and *is* enforced. The Albion Basin road continues for 2.5 miles and reaches the Albion Basin Campground and Cecret Lake trailhead after 11.0 miles.

ROUTES

■ **13.1 West Ridge via Snowbird and Peruvian Gulch, Class 2**

From Snowbird Resort Trailhead: 7.5 miles RT; 2,950 feet

A Snowbird area map may be helpful, as trails and roads are subject to change. The Peruvian Gulch trail is a popular descent for those who ride the tram to the top of Hidden Peak. The approach leaves from the tram-loading area and follows Dick Bass Highway trail to the top of Wilbre Ski Lift. The 4wd road forks here. The right fork leads into Gad Valley. The left fork turns east and crosses into Peruvian Gulch to join the road ascending from the Cliff Lodge area of Snowbird. Both routes join at 8,800 feet near the top of Peruvian ski lift. Continue ascending the wide 4wd road as it winds up to the ridge directly east of Hidden Peak. Upon reaching the ridge at 10,700 feet,

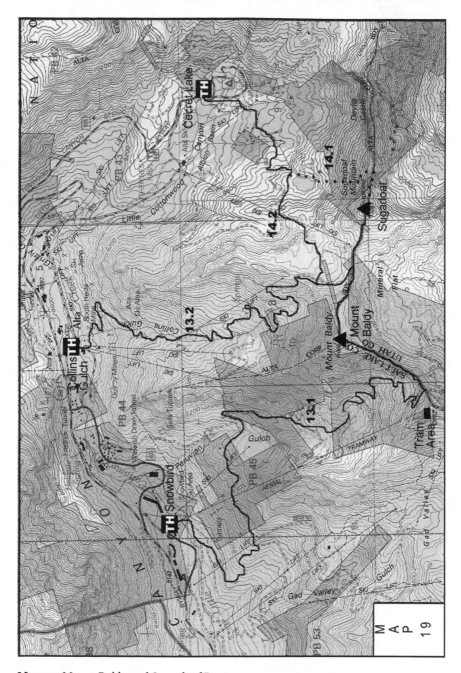

MAP 19. *Mount Baldy and Sugarloaf Routes*

leave the 4wd road east of Hidden Peak. A climber's trail stays along the ridge. Gently climb 370 feet to reach the top of Mount Baldy.

▦ 13.2 East Ridge via Alta and Collins Gulch, Class 2

From Cecret Lake Trailhead: 3.2 miles RT; 1,670 feet

From Collins Gulch Trailhead: 6.6 miles RT; 2,670 feet

Leave the parking area and begin climbing the 4wd service road between the Collins and Wildcat ski lifts. Climb the road as it makes two long switchbacks into the gulch. Near the base of Germania ski lift, the road forks. The right fork leads west to the top of Wildcat ski lift. The left fork continues climbing east to the top of Germania ski lift. Take the left fork and climb 2.5 miles to the top of a spur ridge. This is the top of Germania ski lift at 10,300 feet. After a few yards connect with the Sugarloaf service road that has been climbing from Albion Basin. Climb the remaining 200 feet to reach the Sugarloaf/ Mount Baldy saddle at 10,500 feet after 2.9 miles. This saddle can also be reached by an approach from Cecret Lake (see Route 14.2 for description). Climb right (west) from the 10,500-foot saddle between Sugarloaf and Mount Baldy. A climber's trail leads through a small cliff band at the west end of the saddle. Climb through the cliff band to reach the gentle, grassy slopes above the cliffs. Contour slightly north then west to reach Mount Baldy's summit at 11,068 feet after 3.3 miles.

14. Sugarloaf Mountain – 11,051 feet

See maps on pages 72 and 83

Sugarloaf is a gentle giant. The ridges are rounded. Approaches are short and routes are non-technical. Sugarloaf offers unique views of rugged Devil's Castle to the east. Sugarloaf is often overlooked, but it should never be forgotten.

TRAILHEADS

▦ Collins Gulch

See page 81 for description

Left to right: *Devil's Castle and Sugarloaf viewed from Germania Pass*

■ **Cecret (Secret) Lake**

See page 82 for description

ROUTES

■ **14.1 East Ridge via Cecret Lake, Class 2**

From Cecret Lake Trailhead: 4.0 miles RT; 1,650 feet

Leave the Albion Basin campground and hike west around the camp-ground area. This trail is an interpretive trail and has signs along the way. Naturally, it is a popular hike. Follow the trail as it crosses a stream and makes two switchbacks climbing the rocky slope below the lake. Climb the last switchback to reach the northeast edge of the lake at 9,920 feet after 0.75 miles. From the northeast edge of Cecret Lake, look for a faint trail through the willows on the east side of the lake. It is about 15 feet from the edge of the lake when the lake is full. Cross the east side of the lake staying near the water's edge and reach the south end of the lake. A climber's trail begins climbing through broken ledges. Find the trail and climb steeply for 600 feet to reach the saddle between Devil's Castle and Sugarloaf at 10,760 feet. Turn right (west) and gain the east ridge of Sugarloaf. Climb the remaining 500 feet along the gentle, Class 2 east ridge to the summit.

■ **14.2 West Ridge via Cecret Lake, Class 2**

From Cecret Lake Trailhead & Sugarloaf Road: 4.5 miles RT; 1,650 feet

From Collins Gulch Trailhead: 6.6 miles RT: 2,650 feet

Leave the Albion Basin campground and hike west around the campground area. This trail is an interpretive trail and has signs along the way. Naturally, it is a popular hike. Follow the trail as it crosses a stream and makes two switchbacks climbing the rocky slope below the lake. Climb the last switchback to reach the northeast edge of the lake at 9,920 feet after 0.7 miles. From the north end of Cecret Lake, a climber's trail leaves from the northwestern edge. Continue hiking left (west) under the Sugarloaf ski lift to gain the Sugarloaf service road. Turn left (south) and follow the road a short distance until it turns west again. Follow the road as it connects with the road that has ascended Collins Gulch to Germania Pass. Gain the saddle between Sugarloaf and Mount Baldy at 10,500 feet. Alternatively, the 10,500-foot saddle can be reached via Collins Gulch (see Route 13.2 for description). From the 10,500-foot saddle between Mount Baldy and Sugarloaf, turn left (east). The west ridge is sprinkled with trees. Meander through the trees on the boulder-covered ridge and climb the remaining 550 feet to Sugarloaf's summit.

■ **The Bullion Traverse, Class 4**

From Cecret Lake Trailhead & exit via Red Pine: 11.5 miles total; 4,500 feet gain & 6,200 feet loss

This is the most efficient way to climb five eleveners. A car shuttle is required for this traverse from White Pine trailhead to Cecret Lake trailhead. Leave the Cecret Lake trailhead at 9,400 feet and hike to Cecret Lake. Contour around the left (east) side of the lake and climb 600 feet to gain the ridge east of Sugarloaf Peak at 10,650 feet. Ascend Sugarloaf's east ridge to Sugarloaf's summit after 2.0 miles. Descend Sugarloaf's west ridge to reach the saddle between Sugarloaf and Mount Baldy at 10,500 feet. Ascend Mount Baldy's east ridge to Mount Baldy's summit. Descend a good trail to the saddle east of Hidden

The Bullion Traverse viewed from American Fork Twin Peaks

Cecret Lake and Albion Basin

Peak at 10,800 feet. Contour south under Hidden Peak and the tram area at 10,800 feet. Engage the knife-edge ridge and climb 630 feet to American Fork Twin Peaks' east summit at 11,433 feet. Lose 130 feet, then climb 190 feet on open tundra to American Fork Twin Peaks' west summit at 11,489 feet after 4.5 miles. Traverse west from the summit and lose 290 feet to reach the saddle between Red Top

Mountain and American Fork Twin Peaks' west summit. Climb 150 feet to Red Top Mountain's summit. Turn southwest and drop 700 feet on the Class 2 ridge to the saddle between Red Top Mountain and Red Baldy. From the 10,550-foot saddle, the climbing begins again. Climb the Class 4 northeast ridge of Red Baldy and reach the summit after 5.5 miles. Continue a short, Class 3 traverse to Red Baldy's west summit. Transition off the ridge to an open area left (south) of the ridge and descend to the Red Baldy/White Baldy saddle at 10,680 feet. Climb 700 feet along the east ridge of White Baldy to reach the summit after 6.5 miles. Descend the Class 3 west ridge of White Baldy and reach the low point along the ridge at 10,500 feet after 7.0 miles. Turn right (north) and begin descending to upper Red Pine Lake. Or ascend 200 feet in 0.5 miles along the ridge and connect with the climber's trail coming up from Red Pine Lake for the Pfeifferhorn. Descend to Red Pine Lake and continue 3.4 miles to White Pine trailhead.

4

Timpanogos Group

Introduction

Mount Timpanogos Wilderness Area shares its northern border with
Lone Peak Wilderness Area. The Timpanogos Wilderness Area is situ-
ated between American Fork Canyon on the north and Provo Canyon
on the south. There are two peaks in the Timpanogos Group, Mount
Timpanogos and Provo Peak. They could not be more opposite from
one another. "Timp," as it is called by locals, is an impressive and popular mountain. It has two highly developed trailheads with beauti-
fully maintained trails. Provo Peak is not well known, does not have a
trailhead, and does not have a maintained trail. Timpanogos commands its own guidebook while Provo Peak is not in many guidebooks. Both are unique in their own way and both will challenge you.

The north face of Mount Timpanogos

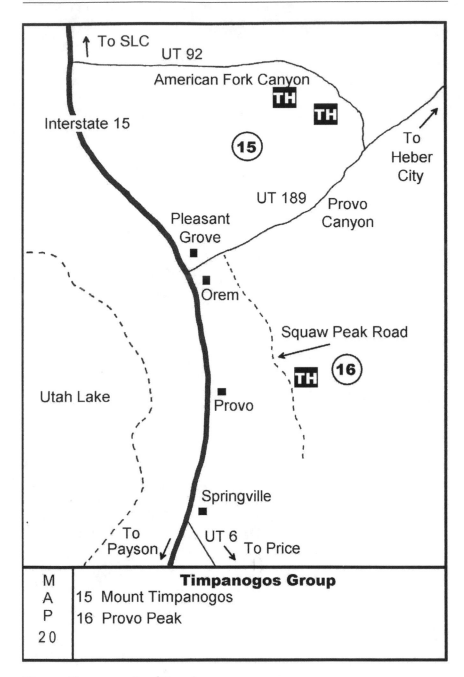

MAP 20. *Timpanogos Road Overview*

15. Mount Timpanogos – 11,749 feet

See maps on pages 92 and 94

Mount Timpanogos is the second highest peak in the Wasatch, second only to Mount Nebo. "Timp" is easily the most popular mountain in the state of Utah. Timp towers over the Provo, Orem, and Pleasant Grove area and *is* the skyline. It rises 7,000 feet from the valley floor and will draw your gaze toward it. Timp has a rich history which is worth reading about in other books. Timp is a huge mountain extending almost seven miles in a north/south direction and has several unnamed points over 11,000 feet. The main peak rises to 11,749 feet. The well-maintained trails have trapped the unwary over the years and Timp has claimed many lives. Snow and ice can block easy progress along the trail, particularly on the upper rocky sections. An ice axe and crampons are recommended for any ascents where snow may be encountered. Snow bridges are another very real hazard. Water runs beneath the snow creating bridges. Sunlight weakens the bridges and they collapse when walked upon. Understand the conditions on Timpanogos before climbing and prepare accordingly.

TRAILHEADS

▪ Timpooneke

At 7,360 feet, this trailhead provides access to both the north and south ridges. The north ridge is usually climbed from the Timpooneke trailhead. From I-15 south of Salt Lake City and north of Provo, take Exit 284 for the town of Alpine. Turn east and reach American Fork Canyon and a fee booth at 9.8 miles. The vehicle fee of $3 in 2005 is subject to change. Continue east and pass the north fork junction and Highway 144 after 12.2 miles. Continue straight (east) and follow signs for Aspen Grove. Reach the sign for Timpooneke Campground at 15.6 miles. Turn right (southwest) and continue a short distance through the campground to reach the trailhead after 15.9 miles. Parking is on the left (south) side of the road. Parking may be challenging on weekends during the summer due to Timpanogos' popularity.

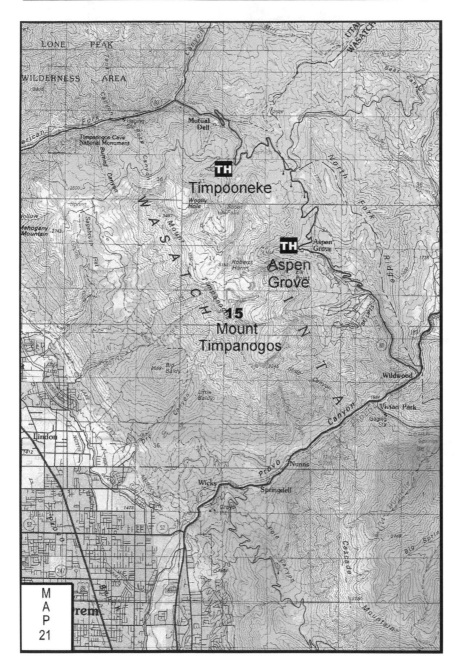

MAP 21. *Timpanogos Trailhead Overview*

Local residents of Mount Timpanogos Wilderness

■ Aspen Grove

This trailhead is at 6,850 feet and provides access to both the north and south ridges. If approaching from the north, leave I-15 south of Salt Lake City and north of Provo. Take Exit 284 for the town of Alpine. Turn east and reach American Fork Canyon and a fee booth at 9.8 miles. The vehicle fee of $3 is subject to change. Continue east and pass the north fork junction and Highway 144 after 12.2 miles. Go straight (east) and follow signs for Aspen Grove. Reach a sign for Timpooneke Campground at 15.6 miles. Continue on the main road a little over 6 miles to reach Aspen Grove trailhead after 22.0 miles. There is a large parking lot immediately west of the fee booth. The trailhead is well marked and leaves from the north end of the parking area.

If approaching from the south, exit I-15 north of the town of Orem at Exit 269. Turn east onto Highway 52 and travel 3.7 miles to reach Highway 189 and Provo Canyon. Continue east on Highway 189 to

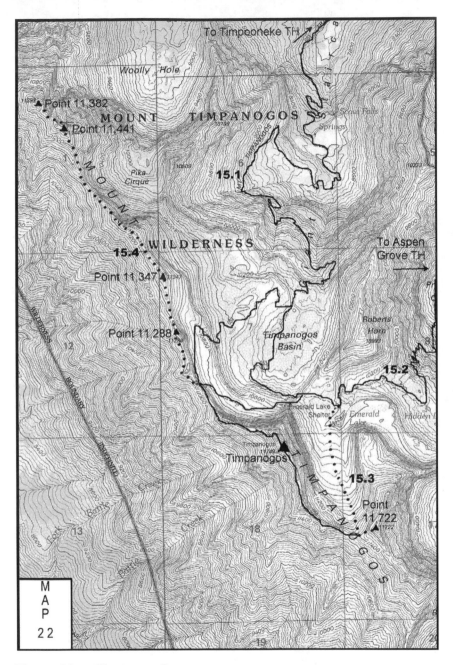

MAP 22. *Mount Timpanogos Routes*

reach the junction with Highway 92 after 10.4 miles. Turn left (north) onto Highway 92. Pass Sundance Ski Resort area and reach Aspen Grove trailhead after 15.2 miles. The trailhead is immediately past the fee booth.

ROUTES

■ **15.1 Timpooneke, Class 2**

From Timpooneke Trailhead: 18.0 miles RT; 4,400 feet

This slightly longer approach to Mount Timpanogos summit is easily justified. The Timpooneke approach is a beautiful, rewarding climb up what is known as the Giant Staircase through lush meadows filled with wildflowers. During most of the summer, several waterfalls beg to be photographed. This trail is popular and crowded on weekends. Leave the parking area and climb gradually to reach a junction with a trail branching east to Scout Falls after 1.0 miles at 8,080 feet. The trail is never steep and continues making switchbacks to reach Middle Basin. Middle Basin is marked by avalanche debris. Make several long switchbacks including one long switchback on the western side of the basin. Climb this long switchback and begin making shorter switchbacks, eventually ending up on the east side of the basin. At 10,000 feet, climb into the open basin area under the impressive 1,600-foot north face of Mount Timpanogos. A trail branches to the right (west) and leads to a toilet and the site of an old B-52 plane crash site. Stay left (south) and climb another 100 feet to reach another junction. The left fork leads to Emerald Lake and the trail from Aspen Grove. Take the right fork and enter an open meadow area. The saddle is visible to the west. Climb the switchbacks to reach the saddle at 11,030 feet. Turn left (south) on the climber's trail and continue ascending. Climb short switchbacks through a short cliff area. Above the short switchbacks at 11,350 feet, the summit of Timpanogos is visible. Contour east and climb the remaining 400 feet to the summit. The summit is marked by a metal hut with a triangular roof. The summit register is located inside the hut.

South Timpanogos viewed from main summit

■ 15.2 Aspen Grove, Class 2

From Aspen Grove Trailhead: 16.0 miles RT; 4,900 feet

The south ridge is usually climbed from the Aspen Grove trailhead. From the north end of the parking area, hike west. The first mile of the trail is paved and leads to a spectacular waterfall. Make several short switchbacks as the trail begins climbing into Primrose Cirque. Make a 0.4-mile-long switchback between 7,800 and 8,200 feet. At 8,200 feet switchback toward Primrose Cirque for another mile before beginning relentless, short switchbacks. Climb the short switchbacks to enter Hidden Lakes Basin at 9,800 feet. Contour right (west) and climb 500 feet to reach Emerald Lake at 10,300 feet after 6.4 miles. Look south and choose your line of ascent. Continue straight (west) to intersect the trail ascending from Timpooneke trailhead. From Emerald Lake, conditions will dictate your ascent on boulders, snow, or a combination. Snow bridges are a hazard, and caution should be exercised while making this ascent. Climb 1,000 feet in 0.8 miles to reach the ridge at 11,300 feet. Turn right (west) and begin an ascending traverse for 0.8 miles northwest on a good trail to gain Timpanogos's main summit at 11,749 feet.

North Timpanogos viewed from main summit

▪ 15.3 Unnamed Point 11,722, Class 2

From 11,300 Saddle: 0.4 miles RT; 420 feet gain/loss

This unnamed point is sometimes referred to as "South" Timpanogos. From the 11,300-foot saddle south of Timp's main summit, turn left (east). Climb gentle, Class 2 terrain for 0.2 miles to reach Unnamed Point 11,722.

▪ 15.4 Unnamed Points 11,288, 11,347, 11,441, & 11,383, Class 2

From 11,030 Saddle: 4.0 miles RT; 2,200 feet gain/loss

From the 11,030-foot saddle north of Timp's main summit, turn right (north). A faint trail contours around Point 11,288 to the left (west). Leave the trail briefly to reach Point 11,288 and then regain the trail at 11,050 north of Point 11,288 after 0.4 miles. Traverse and climb gently to reach Point 11,347 after 0.8 miles. Traverse a short distance at 11,300 feet before dropping to reach the saddle south of Point 11,441 at 10,800 feet after 1.4 miles. Unnamed Point 11,441 is sometimes referred to as "North" Timp. Begin climbing Class 2 slopes steeply to reach Point 11,441 after 1.8 miles. Lose 180 feet before climbing the final 100 feet to reach Point 11,383 after 2.0 miles.

Provo Peak viewed from Squaw Peak Road

16. Provo Peak – 11,068 feet

See maps on pages 99 and 101

Provo Peak is a relatively unknown and unassuming peak. Overshadowed by the more popular Mount Timpanogos to the north and Mount Nebo to the south, it hides on the ridge east of the town for which it is named. Access to Provo Peak is from the west and it is the only trailhead that requires a 4wd vehicle to reach. It is ironic that the approach is rough for such a gentle peak.

TRAILHEAD

▪ **Squaw Peak Road**

From I-15 approximately 35 miles south of Salt Lake City near the town of Orem, take Exit 272. Turn onto Highway 52 and travel east toward Provo Canyon, merging with Highway 189 after 3.7 miles. Continue east in Provo Canyon. A sign for Squaw Peak Road is on the right (south) after 5.5 miles. Turn right onto the paved Squaw Peak Road and measure from this point. Reach a junction after 4.0 miles and turn left (south). The pavement ends after 4.4 miles. The road is passable for two-wheel-drive (2wd) vehicles and is well maintained.

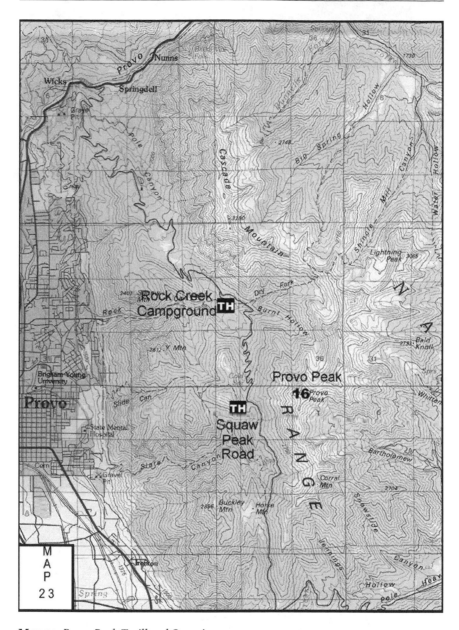

MAP 23. *Provo Peak Trailhead Overview*

Continue another 5.0 miles to reach Rock Creek Campground after 9.4 miles. The road requires 4wd or high-clearance 2wd vehicles from Rock Creek Campground for the next 3.9 miles to the trailhead. Parking is available for 2wd vehicles at Rock Creek Campground at 6,900 feet. Walking or driving, continue climbing along the road and reach a series of switchbacks. At the top of the switchbacks, the valley comes into view to the south as the road turns sharply east. This is the trailhead after 13.3 miles. The trailhead is unmarked. Park in a small turnout to the right (west).

ROUTE

■ 16.1 West Slopes, Class 2

From 4wd area of Squaw Peak Road: 2.6 miles RT; 2,970 feet

From 2wd parking at Rock Creek Campground: 10.4 miles RT; 4,150 feet

This trailhead is at 8,100 feet and provides access to Provo Peak's west slopes. From the parking area, gain a visual of your route to the east. There are several variations to the beginning of this route. The most sensible and direct route will be described. From the parking area, cross the road and find a trail leading through small quaking aspen trees. The trail quickly fades but stays right (south) of the thickest trees. Follow the trail as it gains an erosion terrace that was constructed in the early 1900s. Gain the terrace and turn left (north). Contour on a faint trail as it climbs in a northeasterly direction for 0.4 miles. The west ridge is always on your right to the east. Leave the terrace and climb southeast and then east through open meadows and small quaking aspen trees until gaining the west ridge after 0.6 miles. The ridge gets steeper and climbs through one last stand of quaking aspen trees between 9,200 and 9,400 feet. A faint trail can be picked up through these trees. Reaching the top of the trees after 0.8 miles, a faint but more visible trail welcomes you. Gain 1,500 feet in the next 0.5 miles to reach Provo Peak's summit at 11,068 feet.

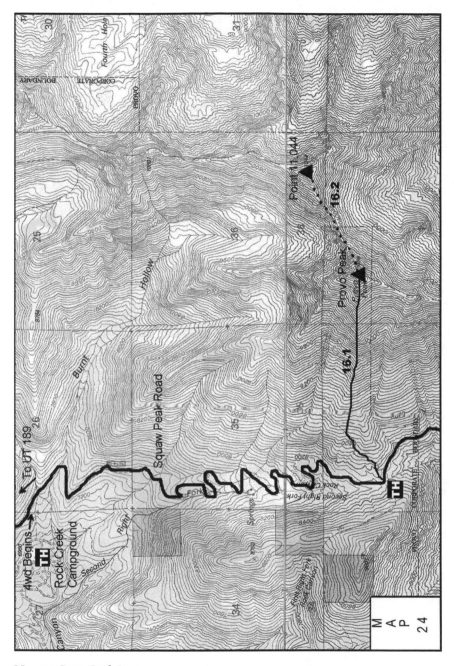

MAP 24. *Provo Peak Routes*

■ **16.2 Unnamed Point 11,044, Class 2**

From Provo Peak's summit: 1.4 miles RT; 1200 feet

Unnamed Point 11,044 is sometimes referred to as "East" Provo Peak. From Provo Peak's summit, begin descending east. Stay on the right (south) side of the ridge to avoid cliffs. Drop to the 10,420-foot saddle in the next 0.25 miles. Traverse slightly east, then resume climbing, reaching Unnamed Point 11,044 after 0.7 miles.

5

Nebo Group

Introduction

The Nebo Wilderness Group rises majestically 70 miles south of Salt Lake City near the town of Nephi. The peaks in this group rise more than 7,000 feet above the valley floor and are neck-breaking when viewed from I-15. The three summits of Mount Nebo are the main attraction for climbers, but the Nebo Wilderness is very popular with hikers, hunters, and sightseers alike. An autumn drive on the Nebo Scenic Byway on the east side of the range will convert you to this area.

17. North Peak – 11,174 feet

See maps on pages 106 and 107

North Peak hides in the shadow of the north summit of Mount Nebo. It is a short side-trip from the north Nebo approach trail. It is named, it is above 11,000 feet, and it is included for that reason.

TRAILHEAD

■ **North Peak**

This trailhead is at 9,020 feet and provides access to North Peak and the north approach to Mount Nebo. Do not confuse the North Peak trail with Monument trailhead and the Nebo Bench trail. North Peak trail is 0.4 miles north of the parking area for Nebo Bench trail at Monument trailhead. If approaching from the north, take I-15 south of Salt Lake City about 40 miles to the town of Payson. Exit the interstate at Payson (Exit 250) and begin measuring as you cross under

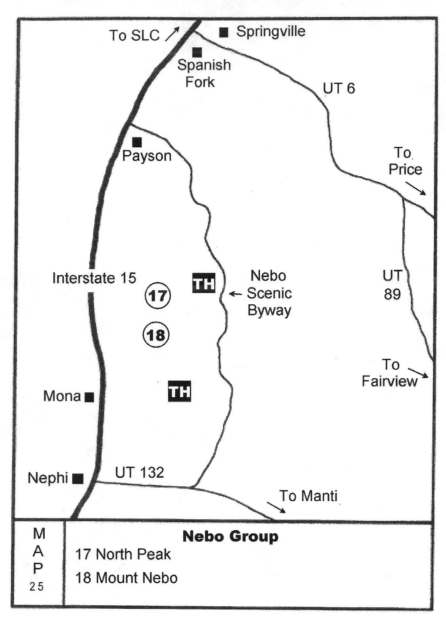

MAP 25. *Nebo Group Road Overview*

Left to right: *the three summits of Mount Nebo and North Peak*

North Peak from the east

the interstate. Go south through the town of Payson for 0.7 miles and turn left (east) at the stoplight (100 North). Continue to 600 East at 1.1 miles and turn right (south) onto the Nebo Scenic Byway. Continue on the Nebo Scenic Byway for 24 miles and reach Monument trailhead after 25.2 miles.

If approaching from the south at the town of Nephi, take Exit 225 from I-15. Drive east on Highway 132 for 4.8 miles to reach the turnoff

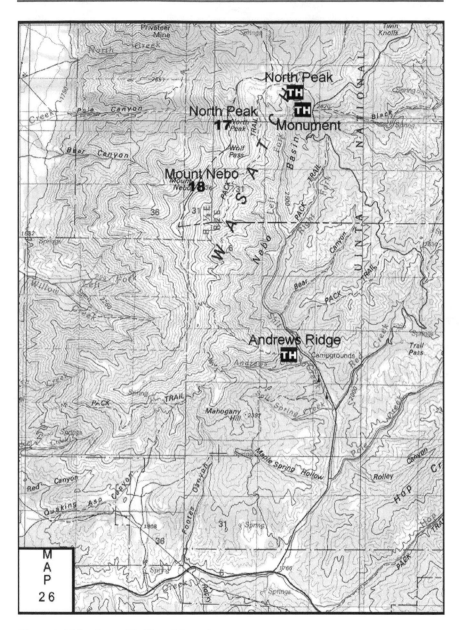

MAP 26. *Nebo Group Trailhead Overview*

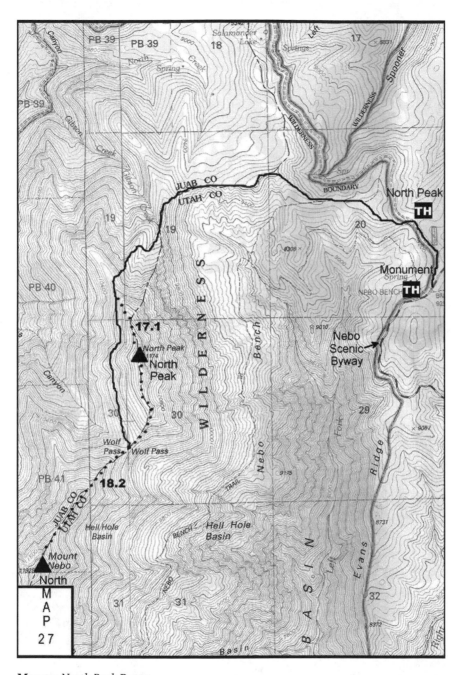

MAP 27. *North Peak Route*

for the Nebo Scenic Byway. Turn left (north) and reach Monument trailhead after 18.1 miles. Parking for 2wd vehicles is available at Monument trailhead. North Peak trailhead is 0.4 miles to the north along the Mona Pole Road, which is on the right at the entrance to Monument trailhead. Turn right (north) onto Mona Pole Road and continue for 0.4 miles. Cross the cattle guard and park here.

APPROACH

■ **North Peak**

From the parking area near the cattle guard on Mona Pole Road at 9,020 feet, begin climbing the trail to the west. Stay near the cattle fence initially as it climbs along the north bench gaining 400 feet. Traverse west on the well-defined trail as it loses 150 feet of elevation just gained. Continue west and begin climbing through stands of trees to reach a northeast-facing drainage. Climb along the left (south) side of this drainage initially, then make a sharp switchback to the right (north) and cross the drainage. Climb steeply along the north side of the drainage through intermittent trees to reach the ridge at 10,540 feet after 2.5 miles. Views open up to the west and the valley below.

North Mount Nebo from the North Peak approach

The north ridge of North Peak

■ 17.1 North Ridge, Class 2

From North Peak Trailhead: 6.0 miles RT; 2,150 feet

From Monument Trailhead: 6.8 miles RT; 2,200 feet

From the ridge north of North Peak at 10,540 feet, turn left (south). Follow the faint trail along the ridge until it leaves the ridge to continue the approach to North Mount Nebo. A faint climber's trail continues climbing along the ridge. Climb 600 feet along the open ridge as views of North Mount Nebo to the south inspire you, reaching North Peak's summit at 11,174 feet. The hearty may choose to continue to North Mount Nebo. If you are one of them, descend down the Class 2 south ridge 0.3 miles to Wolf Pass and join the North Mount Nebo Route (See Route 18.2) at 10,600 feet.

18. Mount Nebo – 11,928 feet

See maps on pages 106 and 111

Mount Nebo carries the honor of being the highest peak in the Wasatch Mountains. It stands singular and unique, and one summit

The south approach with North Mount Nebo in the distance

alone cannot contain this monarch. Nebo is a biblical name and has religious meaning for many. Its three summits and scenic approaches have converted many.

TRAILHEADS

▓ Andrews Ridge

This trailhead is at 6,500 feet and provides access to Nebo's south route. From the town of Nephi 80 miles south of Salt Lake City, take Exit 225 from I-15. Drive east on Highway 132 for 4.8 miles to reach the turnoff for the Nebo Scenic Byway. Turn left (north) and reach the turnoff for Bear Canyon Picnic Area after 8.1 miles. Turn left (west) and reach a hiker's sign after 9.3 miles. Turn left into the small trailhead parking area. The trail leaves from the west end of the parking area.

▓ North Peak

See page 103 for description

APPROACHES

▓ Andrews Ridge

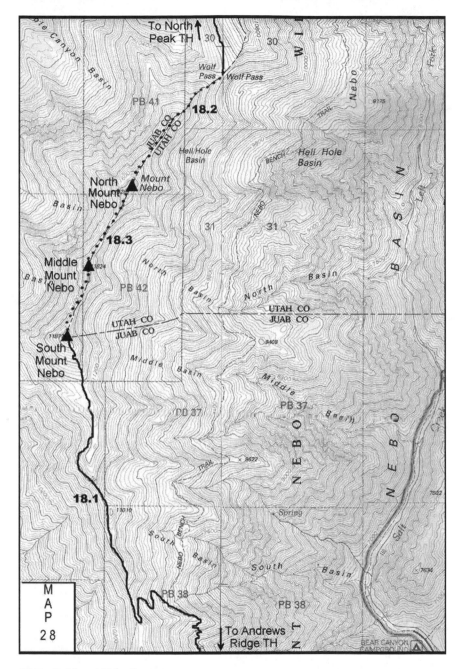

MAP 28. *Mount Nebo Routes*

This approach is long and can be brutally hot in the summer months. Begin climbing on the well-marked trail from the west end of the parking area. Reach the first of several switchbacks after 0.5 miles. Climb the switchbacks to reach Andrews Ridge after 2.0 miles. Continue climbing and making switchbacks along Andrews Ridge for another 2.5 miles. Leave Andrews Ridge at 9,450 feet as the trail drops along its north side. There are some small campsites just off the trail at this point. Continue climbing north steeply for 1.3 miles up three switchbacks to reach the ridge at 10,550 feet. A wooden sign marks where the trail from the west up Willow Creek joins the Andrews Ridge trail. The Willow Creek trail is another approach to the top of Mount Nebo that begins east of the town of Mona and offers an alternative.

■ North Peak

See page 108 for description

ROUTES

■ 18.1 South Ridge via Andrews Ridge, Class 2

From Andrews Ridge Trailhead: 16.0 miles RT; 5,350 feet

Left to right: *South, Middle, and North Mount Nebo*

From the main ridge south of Mount Nebo at 10,550 feet, turn right (north). The three peaks of Mount Nebo come into view to the north. From this point Nebo's south summit is 1.7 miles away and the north summit is 2.7 miles away. Contour along the ridge, gaining elevation gradually. The trail is braided in places, and your choice of trails will depend on the presence of residual snow along the ridge. After 1.3 miles reach a small, flat area south of Nebo's south summit. Climb Class 2 slopes for the last 500 feet to reach the summit at 11,877 feet. A plaque from the Wasatch Mountain Club marks the summit. You may return to Andrews Ridge trailhead or begin the one-mile-long Nebo Traverse (see Route 18.3) and exit via North Peak trailhead. A car shuttle is required to return to Andrews Ridge trailhead.

18.2 North Ridge, Class 2

From North Peak Trailhead: 10.0 miles RT; 3,550 feet

From the main ridge north of North Mount Nebo and North Peak at 10,540 feet, turn south. Your objective, North Mount Nebo, looms to the south. Follow the trail along the ridge and begin contouring along the west slopes of North Peak. Climb 230 feet before descending 170 feet to reach Wolf Pass at 10,600 feet. Resume climbing steeply 850 feet to reach point 11,440 north of Nebo's north summit. The remaining route is clearly visible from this point. As you climb along the ridge, the drop to the west is dramatic. Stay along the ridge until 100 feet below the summit. Do an ascending traverse along the northeast face to reach North Mount Nebo at 11,928 feet. You may return to North Peak trailhead or begin the one-mile-long Nebo Traverse (see Route 18.3) and exit via Andrews Ridge trailhead. A car shuttle is required to return to North Peak trailhead.

18.3 The Nebo Traverse, Class 3–4

From Andrews Ridge Trailhead: 18.0 miles RT; 7,050 feet

From North Peak Trailhead: 12.0 miles RT; 4,750 feet

Most people choose to do this traverse in one day starting with Nebo's north summit, traversing to the south, and then returning over

The north route to North Mount Nebo

The Nebo Traverse viewed from North Mount Nebo

Nebo's north summit. The traverse is 1.0 miles and requires Class 3–4 climbing depending upon your line of ascent. From Nebo's north summit you will notice a trail that drops down the west slopes. This is a less-than-ideal trail, but it does bypass the most difficult portion of the ridge between the north and middle summits. If you came to

North Mount Nebo viewed from the south

climb, then stay along the ridge for a Class 4 descent 700 feet to the saddle between Nebo's middle and north summits. The rock along the ridge is unstable in places and is more easily ascended than descended. Either way, don't trust any of the rock. A safer descent is along the east side of the ridge in Class 3 terrain. Contour 10 to 20 feet under the ridge on Class 3 ledges to gain the ridge again slightly above the saddle. From the 11,200-foot saddle take a deep breath. Climb along the ridge 600 feet toward Nebo's middle summit on Class 2 talus. There is a trail visible in most places along the ridge. Stay close to the ridge and climb to Nebo's middle summit at 11,824 feet. The traverse to Nebo's south summit at 11,877 feet is 0.25 miles and primarily Class 3, but quickly turns to Class 4 if you get off route. Lose 200 feet to gain the saddle between the middle and south summits at 11,650 feet. Begin the crux of the traverse. Generally, it is easier to traverse near the ridge or just off the ridge on the west side. The east side is marked with cliffs and loose, treacherous rubble. Some up-and-down climbing will be required to negotiate along the ridge. Pick your way carefully. The final hundred yards to Nebo's south summit is Class 2.

Terminology

Bench: A shelf or terrace.

Boulderfield: A large area of boulders.

Bushwhack: To navigate a path through thick trees, brush or under-growth.

Cairn: A pile of stones to mark a direction of travel.

Cirque: A deep steep-walled basin on a mountain usually forming the blunt end of a valley.

Cornice: An overhanging mass or ice or snow usually on a ridge.

Contour: A fairly level traverse.

Exposure: A euphemism for the amount of air beneath your feet.

Granite: A very hard, natural igneous rock. Most of the white-colored rock in the Wasatch is granite.

Headwall: Usually a rocky cliff area at the top of a basin or drainage.

Piton: A spike, wedge, or peg driven into rock used for mountain climbing protection.

Quartzite: A compact granular rock. The red-colored rock found in the Wasatch is quartzite.

Ridge: An elongated elevation. Usually the top of the intersection between canyons, drainages, and between mountain peaks.

Saddle: Usually the low point on a ridge between two points or peaks.

Scramble: Climbing using all four appendages.

Scree: An accumulation of loose stones or rocky debris lying on a slope or at the base of a hill or cliff.

Slab: A solid section of rock.

Snowbridge: A bridge of snow remaining after underlying snow has melted.

Snowfield: A broad area of snow.

Snowpack: A seasonal accumulation of snow.

Switchback: A point in a trail that marks a change of direction.

Talus: A slope formed especially by an accumulation of rock debris, or rock debris at the base of a cliff.

Traverse: Fairly level horizontal hiking or scrambling between two points or peaks.

Tundra: A level of treeless terrain above tree-line in mountainous areas.

References

Salt Lake Ranger District
Manages Wasatch-Cache National Forest including Twin Peaks and Lone Peak Wilderness areas.
6944 South 3000 East
Salt Lake City, UT 84121
(801) 733-2660
M–F 8:00am–4:30pm
http://www.fs.fed.us/r4/wcnf/unit/slrd/index.shtml

Wasatch–Cache Recreational Information
3285 East 3300 South (inside REI)
Salt Lake City, UT 84109
Tu–Sa 10:30am–7pm
Pleasant Grove Ranger District
Manages Uinta National Forest and Timpanogos Wilderness area. Also manages Squaw Peak Road and Provo Peak area.
390 North 100 East
Pleasant Grove, UT 84062
(801) 785-3563
http://www.fs.fed.us/r4/uinta/

Spanish Fork Ranger District
Manages Uinta National Forest and Nebo Wilderness area.
44 West 400 North
Spanish Fork, UT 84660
(801) 798-3571
http://www.fs.fed.us/r4/uinta/

Statewide Road Conditions 1-800-492-2400
UDOT Road Closure Hotline (801) 975-4838
http://www.udot.utah.gov/public/road_conditions.htm

Avalanche and Backcountry Conditions
Office (801) 524-5304
M–F 4:00am–noon
Recording (801) 364-1581
http://www.utahavalanchecenter.com

Campgrounds

The main campgrounds are listed below:

TABLE 3. *Campgrounds*

CAMPGROUND	CANYON
Jordan Pine	Big Cottonwood
The Spruces	Big Cottonwood
Redman	Big Cottonwood
Tanners Flat	Little Cottonwood
Albion Basin	Little Cottonwood
Granite Flat	American Fork
Little Mill	American Fork
Timpooneke	American Fork
Ponderosa	Nebo Scenic Byway

Campground Reservations 1-877-444-6777
http://www.ReserveUSA.com

TABLE 4. *Route Summaries*

RTE	DESCRIPTION	CLASS	FROM TRAILHEAD	MILES RT	ELEVATION	PAGE
1.1	Twin Southeast	3-4	Broads Fork	9.0	5,130	18
1.2	Twin North	3	Broads Fork	8.0	5,130	20
1.3	Twin West	3	Deaf Smith	9.0	6,130	20
2.1	Sunrise East	3	Tanners Gulch	3.6	4,075	22
2.2	Sunrise West	3	Broads Fork	8.0	5,075	24
3.1	Dromedary West	3	Broads Fork	8.0	4,910	26
3.1	Dromedary West	3	Tanners Gulch	3.6	3,910	26
3.2	Dromedary East	3	Broads Fork	8.0	4,910	26
4.1	Superior East	3	Cardiff Pass	5.0	2,600	30
5.1	Lone North	4	Big Willow	11.0	6,150	42
5.2	Lone West	4	Orson Smith	12.0	6,450	43
5.3	Lone West	4	Draper Ridge	13.6	5,950	43
5.3	Lone West	4	Jacobs Ladder	12.6	5,650	43
5.4	Lone South	3	Schoolhouse	10.5	5,950	45
6.1	South Thunder West	3	Bells Canyon	12.0	6,025	49
6.2	South Thunder South	2	Schoolhouse	11.5	5,850	49
7.1	North Thunder West	3	Bells Canyon	9.8	6,020	53
7.2	Thunder Traverse	3	Pfeifferhorn White Pine	12.0	4,800G 7,200L	54
7.2	Thunder Traverse	3	Bells Canyon	12.0	6,500	54
8.1	Pfeifferhorn East	3	White Pine	9.0	3,725	56
8.2	Beatout Traverse	3	White Pine	12.5	4,330G 6,800L	58
9.1	White Baldy East	3	White Pine	11.0	3,720	61
9.2	White Baldy West	3	White Pine	10.5	4,120	63
10.1	Box Elder North	2	Dry Creek	14.0	5,650	66
10.1	Box Elder North	2	Deer Creek	9.6	4,300	66
11.1	American Fork Twin North	3	Snowbird	8.0	3,550	73

TABLE 4 (CONT'D.). *Route Summaries*

Rte	Description	Class	From Trailhead	Miles RT	Elevation	Page
11.2	American Fork Twin Northeast	4	Snowbird	8.0	3,400	75
12.1	Red Baldy Northwest	2	White Baldy	8.0	3,570	78
12.2	Red Baldy Northeast	4	White Baldy	8.0	3,570	78
12.3	Red Baldy West	3	White Baldy	9.2	3,570	80
13.1	Baldy West	2	Snowbird	7.5	2,950	82
13.2	Baldy East	2	Collins Gulch	6.6	2,670	84
13.2	Baldy East	2	Cecret Lake	3.2	1,670	84
14.1	Sugarloaf East	2	Cecret Lake	4.0	1,650	85
14.2	Sugarloaf West	2	Cecret Lake	4.5	1,650	86
14.2	Sugarloaf West	2	Collins Gulch	6.6	2,650	86
15.1	Timpanogos Timpooneke	2	Timpooneke	18.0	4,400	95
15.2	Timpanogos Aspen Grove	2	Aspen Grove	16.0	4,900	96
15.3	Point 11,722	2	11,300 saddle	0.4	420	97
15.4	Points 11,000+	2	11,030 saddle	4.0	2,200	97
16.1	Provo West	2	Squaw Peak Rd	2.6	2,970	100
16.1	Provo West	2	Rock Creek CG	10.4	4,150	100
16.2	Point 11,044	2	Provo Summit	1.4	1,200	102
17.1	North Peak North	2	North Peak	6.0	2,150	109
17.1	North Peak	2	Monument	6.8	2,200	109
18.1	Nebo South	2	Andrews Ridge	16.0	5,350	112
18.2	Nebo North	2	North Peak	10.0	3,550	113
18.3	Nebo Traverse	3-4	Andrews Ridge	18.0	7,050	113
18.3	Nebo Traverse	3-4	North Peak	12.0	4,750	113

About the Author

I spent my childhood growing up in the shadow of the Teton Mountains in Idaho. My early years were spent climbing in the Tetons and other mountains in the west. My first adventure was climbing the Grand Teton when I was sixteen years old, and the feeling of accomplishment and exhilaration of climbing stuck with me.

After graduating college in the early 1990s, I moved to Salt Lake City. An office job and otherwise sedentary lifestyle led to poor nutritional habits and subsequent weight gain. The weight gain lead to low energy levels and low self-esteem. In 1996 my father's life was taken prematurely by cancer. I was unhappy and something had to change. It did. In my search to take control of my life, I discovered hiking and remembered my childhood roots. Hiking provided satisfaction and contentment, feelings I had not had for many years. I had found my reason to begin hiking again. I began to hike in the Wasatch Mountains and soon discovered the elation and sense of fulfillment that sitting atop a summit provided. I was addicted. I methodically and systematically hiked every trail and climbed every ridge and mountain along the Wasatch. Somehow, I wanted more. In 1998, I took a two-week-long road trip to the Cascade Mountains, beginning

Randy Winters atop a 14,000-foot peak.

with Mount Shasta in northern California. During my trip I climbed six other Cascade peaks including Mount Hood in Oregon. Realizing some significance to Mount Shasta's elevation of over 14,000 feet, I began researching other high mountains in the western United States. To my delight I discovered seventy peaks above 14,000 feet in the lower United States. That became my goal. In 1999 my quest to climb all the 14,000-foot peaks began, and in less than five years I had attained my goal of climbing all seventy of them—a feat fewer than two hundred people have achieved to date.

Today, I can smile about my first hiking experience in the Wasatch. It occurred on the Mount Olympus trail. At the time I was able to hike 0.5 miles in forty-five minutes before I had to return exhausted! But it was a start. Now, I climb Mount Olympus several times each year from top to bottom in three to four hours as part of my training program. The important thing is to start. Leave now. Go hike! Find a reason to enjoy the outdoors. Hiking and climbing have improved my life physically, emotionally, mentally, and spiritually. At times, life has managed to consign climbing to a lesser priority. However, it has and will always be present and constant in my life. My desire is to provide a motivation for you to find your reason to get outdoors and be active.